CW00802416

Home Farm Cooking

Catherine &
John Pawson

To our mothers
Veronica and Winifred

Home Farm Cooking

Catherine &
John Pawson

Foreword

The Architecture of Home
by Alison Morris

'Architecture is basically a container of something. I hope they will enjoy not so much the teacup, but the tea.'

Yoshio Taniguchi

—

When you first move into a place, it is natural to interrogate the details of the patterns of the life you bring with you. The new architectural setting functions as a lens. For a brief intense period you are mindful of habits and rituals that have become so ingrained they are reflexive. During this time of heightened consciousness — physical and emotional — the details of everyday routines loosen and fragment, before solidifying again in a site-specific hybrid of the familiar, the adaptive and the fresh, with family and friends both observers and participants in this process. And as the narrative of acclimatization advances, so the architecture and landscape settle into their ceaseless cycles of evolution and permanence.

The rural context of Home Farm is a world away from the house in London where John and Catherine have lived for many years. In this Oxfordshire hamlet, the main daily through traffic along the lane comprises horses, tractors, combine harvesters and a local pack of hounds. John and Catherine bought the largely derelict property with the idea of creating somewhere they could bring family and friends together, with space to gather and eat around large tables indoors and out, and where there would be scope for people — particularly their children — to stay for sustained periods and this driving purpose has informed every detail of their vision for the place.

Historically a home farm — also known as a manor farm — was the part of a country estate that was farmed by the landowner or an employed farm manager, to produce food for the estate household, rather than rented out to tenant farmers. A number of generations back, the farm John and Catherine now live in would have supplied the nearby Jacobean country house — including carp for the dining table, there having originally probably been three pools rather than the existing single pond, with the fish moved progressively from the top pool to the cleaner water of the lower one, to make them fit for consumption. In the past, one side of the neighbouring farmhouse served as the laundry for the big house and what is now the Home Farm pantry was used to make cider from the apples in the orchard.

During the weeks and months that followed the purchase of Home Farm, the various buildings and the wider site were gradually cleared of the flotsam left by previous inhabitants — including the giant hogweed that sprouted exuberantly from the derelict pigsties. In the absence of scope for more dramatic transformation, while the planning process ran its course, a form of rudimentary housework was practised, involving the endless wielding of a broom: a gesture of quiet, territorial defiance in the face of a seeming lack of progress, but also the recognizable stirrings of a response to the rhythms of the seasons and the spaces.

Home Farm sits on the edge of a hamlet in the Cotswolds. Set back only marginally from the country lane that runs through the village, its front door opens directly into the farmhouse dining room.

During this period of immersive leaning into the site, a photographer was commissioned to create a meticulous archive of the existing architecture and also document a series of walks in the surrounding countryside, as a medium for orientation, but also as a form of mental geography, allowing the history and geology to imprint themselves deeply. Meantime, a sound artist was using super-sensitive audio equipment to capture aspects of the soundtrack of the place inaudible to the human ear in normal listening conditions, recording the tiniest exhalations of the house and landscape, including — in an act of extreme aural craning — the respiration of the weed in the remaining carp pond. A little later in the project, two photographers based in Germany, who are long-term collaborators of the studio, called by the site and produced a visual response encompassing two extremes of scale — at one end, vast, stitched compositions that allowed all of the many elements of Home Farm's 'disordered farmyard' to be scrutinized within a single image and, at the other, almost forensic studies of found material laid out in orderly grids, from seventeenth-century tacks and hinges, to rusted lengths of chain and agricultural tools.

Accommodation of the rituals of cooking and eating at Home Farm came very much out of this 'total' approach, not as a manifestation of stylistic preferences, but as a commitment to the seamless and intense expression of a way of life. The different way a place makes you feel, according to the weather and the season, has an impact upon what and where you want to eat, in terms of what feels good and appropriate. There are three kitchens in the renovated Home Farm: one in the old farm house (although not in the location of the original farmhouse kitchen), one in the converted barn, and one in the wainhouse. Each of these kitchens has its own individual scale, character and atmosphere, as do the associated eating spaces. The small kitchen in the former farmhouse preserves the traditional model of separate storage with a combined pantry and larder and has an adjacent, intimate dining room, while the open-plan barn, with its refectory-scale table, is the natural location for larger gatherings and celebrations. By virtue of being a self-contained building, the wainhouse provides conditions of perfect semi-seclusion for guests.

Each of the three kitchens at Home Farm has its own physical character and atmosphere — from the calm intimacy of the farmhouse kitchen and the sensory warmth of the wood-panelled kitchen in the wainhouse, to the lofty openness of the barn (overleaf).

John's working process is driven by forensic engagement with the lives of his clients. It is how he understands the character of the architectural space he is making. When an architect designs for his or her own family, the creative dialogue becomes instead, in part at least, a matter of deepening self-knowledge. With no third party to satisfy, the only real constraints are time, money and the tenacity of spirit to keep pushing the thinking. The design of Home Farm was complicated — and enriched — by the fact that there was so much already there. The inherited architecture — a combination of seventeenth, eighteenth, nineteenth and twentieth-century domestic and agricultural structures — was complex and of strong character, and questions of how to draw all the various elements together to make a harmonious formal and functional composition were not quickly or easily resolved. It was important that every room would have its own independent sense of life and atmosphere, but each had also to be integrated within the greater whole. John continues to leave the internal doors open in order that he can look through the vistas, feel the connections and sense the unfolding rhythm, which is evidence of how significant this aspect of the architecture remains to him.

A glimpsed view from the farmhouse sitting room into the link opens into an uninterrupted vista through the stables and barn.

The first time he and Catherine visited the place, John saw the possibilities of closing the gap between the farmhouse and the in-line stone barn, stables and hayloft to create an attenuated sequence of spaces extending nearly 50 metres (164 feet) in length. The contemporary structure that fulfils this function contrasts the transparency of glass with the colour, mass and texture of the surrounding stone and brick. The thickness of the original stone walls — their mass — is visible in every opening. It is a defining gesture in terms of the new composition, but crucially it has been made without losing what had been visually, spatially and atmospherically exhilarating about the original site. The connections between new and old are not smoothed into invisibility. The essential 'disordered' character of the place, with its eccentric accretion of structures, is retained. One remains conscious of the transitions; there is no false historicization. Everywhere the palette is extremely simple and appropriate to what the house has been and what it has quietly become — lime plaster walls and ceilings, elm and concrete floors, exposed elm beams, lime-washed stone walls, raw stainless steel window frames, lintels, sills, hinges and doorknobs and white marble from the Dolomites.

Where the farmhouse windows draw a series of frames, the barn's full-height opening co-opts views and reflections as part of the actual fabric of the place.

In this sort of project, there is often not a single threshold marking the moment of moving in, but rather a series of acts of habitation of increasing breadth and depth. One quickly loses track of the first times — the first time you lit a fire, prepared a meal, spent a night, took a bath. Just as, with equal speed, you also forget the last times — the last time you wished for plumbing not yet installed, unpacked a box, registered an issue for the snagging list. There is significance in the realization that the store cupboards are fully stocked, with perishables as well as nonperishables. Rounds of friends start to come calling and, as a natural consequence, a succession of meals follows, prepared for family, small groups of friends and larger gatherings. On a sunny July day, John's entire studio team was conveyed from north London in a large minibus and ate out under the trees next to the pond. Some months later, shortly after his birth, a first grandchild was brought for a period of peaceful nesting. Several significant birthdays have already been celebrated in the barn. Memories of successive Easters and Christmases are stacking up and a sense of the challenging length and complexity of the narrative of architectural transformation has already begun to recede. In the coming months, beehives will be installed and work will begin on the development of a cutting garden. These are the events that embed people within a place, in a process that is as endless as the cycle of the seasons itself.

Preface

Ten years ago John and I bravely registered for a charity bike ride from London to Brussels via Amsterdam to support a cause that is very important to us. We spent a summer training in the hills of the Cotswolds, fell in love with the area and decided to start to look for a tiny 'lock up and go' cottage in which to store the bikes and stay for the odd weekend. We had never thought we needed two houses, but at the back of John's mind there had always been the idea of one day designing a place of our own on a plot of land, preferably with a studio to work from.

While idly looking through a property website, I found the dauntingly derelict buildings of Home Farm and took John to visit. The place had been occupied by the large, local farming family for seventy years and was a stranger to modernization — the only electrical outlet was a pre-war, three-pin Bakelite socket. Through the curtains of cobwebs, John immediately saw the potential of the disordered agricultural and farm buildings. It was far from the rose-covered cottage I had dreamed of, nor was it a blank canvas on which we could start from scratch, and anybody we brought to view the place looked deeply sceptical, but it did offer the space we were missing in London. Five years later, we celebrated our first Christmas here.

Home Farm sits on the edge of an escarpment, facing west across Evenlode Valley. The main accommodation consists of a 50-metre (164-foot)-long run of connected buildings — barn, stables and farmhouse — with a kitchen at either end. A third kitchen in the wainhouse overlooks a pond, whose muddy bottom is regularly stirred up by the resident carp. Both the pond and the nearby orchard are several hundred years old and each are wonderful places for eating outside. When people ask why we want three kitchens, the quick answer is that it's never far to go for a coffee. In reality it means that we can split Home Farm into three when the whole family congregates for a sustained period. As things turned out, John didn't get the separate studio he had envisaged, but the calm atmosphere means that he can work anywhere. One of the many ways in which the place has changed my life is that I now cook and entertain regularly; it has presented me with an opportunity to extend my previously narrow culinary repertoire.

Twenty years ago John co-authored a cookbook, *Living and Eating*, with the professional chef and cookery writer Annie Bell. The book has been a cooking bible for me ever since. When Phaidon asked if John might want to do a follow-up, he felt it should be based around what we eat and how we cook at the farm and this time he asked me to collaborate with him. Mealtimes are very important to both of us and, like many, we have become increasingly determined to buy, cook and eat in a way that respects the connection between field and fork. One of our sons has recently become vegan and, while John and I still eat meat and fish, our meals are consciously becoming more plant-based.

I am a home cook. I learnt to cook from my mother, who effortlessly produced nourishing meals for me and my five siblings. John also comes from a large family. Growing up in Yorkshire, his parents were generous and committed hosts and it was rare for there not to be at least one extra place set at the table — Martha Stewart once asked him for his mother's Yorkshire pudding recipe. *Home Farm Cooking* collects together the food we love to cook and eat at the farm: the recipes I use often, some of them my own, others inspired by favourite chefs and cookbooks. I offer them not with the idea that they must be followed slavishly, but as dishes to adapt and tweak. I am extremely grateful to Carole Bamford, Sally Clarke, Skye Gyngell, Prue Leith, Yotam Ottolenghi and Claire Ptak for their permission to reproduce recipes in this book. I am also indebted to many other professional chefs who have inspired me over the years.

If there is a thread that runs through the Home Farm cookbook, it is simple, unpretentious food that is easy to make and that uses seasonal produce. The ingredients are allowed to shine and speak for themselves and this is reflected right through to the way in which a dish is presented at the table or on a plate. Most of the cookware and cutlery that we use is designed by John and manufactured by When Objects Work.

Ultimately, cooking is an act of love and of sharing, of nourishing and nurturing. John and I feel very fortunate to have Home Farm as the setting for all of this.

Spring

'...we should attempt to bring nature, houses and human beings together into a higher unity.'

Ludwig Mies van der Rohe

—

Spring's arrival can feel instantaneous. Overnight there are buds everywhere, bulbs burst into bloom from the dark earth and the daylight gains that have been steadily accumulating since late December are suddenly transformational. The 'firsts' of the year accelerate — our first breakfast outside, the first outing for the punt and, for the hardy, the first swim in the pond. The strengthening sunlight works its way through the various rooms and passages of Home Farm across the course of the day and open windows let in the warming air. In conjunction with the powerful influx of the leafy scents of spring, it is difficult not to feel an upsurge of optimism and possibility.

Spring's lengthening days and rising temperatures tempt us to linger outside, enjoying the soft evening light.

From March the surrounding lanes begin to foam with lacy cow parsley and the damp woodlands fill with lily of the valley, bluebells, snake's head fritillary, forget-me-nots, cowslips and cornflowers. The hedgerows gradually bulk out and all of the fruit trees in the orchard — apple, pear, plum, cherries and quince — come into blossom in the span of what seems like a single week. This is the first garden that we have ever had and we have learned both that the work of a gardener can never be finished and that a garden absorbs an enormous amount of pleasurable time. At this time of year it is filled with jewel-like crocuses, upright hyacinths and that cheeriest of spring bulbs, the daffodil, which we cut and put in vases around the house, along with bunches of multicoloured tulips and branches from the fruit trees studded with blossom. There is a wild flower meadow planted on one side of the pond, where it is too steep to mow, and this begins to thicken with a mix of plant varieties, that will be constantly changing right through to the end of summer. As everything comes to life, the resident heron reappears in the pond from his winter spent in the southern hemisphere and, beyond the confines of Home Farm, the local farmers are up all night, delivering the newborn lambs, which then fill the nearby fields.

On cooler days, there is still the pleasure of lighting a fire in the dining room, but when the weather merits it, there are few greater joys than winding up the glass wall of the barn and feeling the garden become part of the house (overleaf).

Now is the time for foraging and successive pilgrimages are made to Foxholes, just outside the nearby village of Bruern, where ancient woodland sloping down to the River Evenlode is covered with bluebells. Here there is wild garlic growing in the damp shade, which we pound with nuts and olive oil and put into jars, to make a deliciously pungent garlic pesto for serving with pasta, swirling into soups or risottos and smearing onto roasted vegetables. The leaves are wonderful, too, simply added to salads or wilted as a vegetable. There are also young nettle leaves that make a perfect risotto or a very nourishing nettle soup. Although the kitchen garden is still a work in progress — as are the beehives — I nevertheless plant broad (fava) beans, our favourite vegetable, and a multitude of herbs in a flower bed outside the kitchen — chives, vervain, thyme, rosemary, dill, chervil and oregano.

New ingredients arrive at the grocers and farm shops — slender pink stalks of forced rhubarb from Yorkshire, mustard greens, leeks, spinach, sea kale, sprouting broccoli (broccolini) and morels. The appearance of Jersey Royal potatoes towards the end of March is perhaps the first indication that spring is really on its way. As the weeks pass, we look forward to wild and garden rocket (arugula), pea shoots, Swiss chard, spring (collard) greens, sweet herbs, sorrel, radishes, baby carrots and fennel. Artichokes arrive from France, as do soft, lemony goat's cheeses and organic lemons from Sicily and the Amalfi coast, wonderful for a lemon pasta, for flavouring madeleines and for combining with pistachios, polenta (cornmeal) and pomegranates in a favourite cake recipe. April means the start of the short-lived English asparagus season, as well as peas and broad beans. Joys for May include peas and the arrival of Alphonso mangoes from India. There is a rhythmic sense of anticipation, as well as a comforting familiarity, if you cook with the seasons. It provides a sense of life's continuity.

The fresh green scent of wild garlic pesto mixes with the more delicate aroma of early peaches ripening on a sunny window sill.

At Home Farm, there are three family birthdays — including John's — in the spring. These celebrations, along with the warmer weather, are our nudge to move back from the intimacy of the old farmhouse into the loftier proportioned volume of the barn. When we bought the property this barn was filled literally to the rafters with broken-down rusty agricultural machinery. It was divided into three spaces, one of which had the remnants of a fireplace, so we think it used to be lived in by a shepherd or farm worker. We opened everything up, kept the lime-washed rubble walls and the exposed elm beams of the roof structures and inserted a glass wall into the original wooden barn doors. The lower half of this glass wall can be cranked up in a rather Heath Robinson way, bringing the outside in and opening this already expansive space to the outdoors and to the unfettered flow of sunlight in a way that feels quite magical.

The woods and hedgerows around Home Farm fill with wild flowers, which are combined with blooms from the garden to decorate the table for a succession of spring birthday celebrations.

As well as birthdays to look forward to, there is the Easter service at the local medieval village church, which holds its only other services at Christmas and for the harvest festival — opening at other times for the sale of homemade cake and cups of tea to be enjoyed by visitors to the next-door Jacobean house and garden, who sit at tables set amongst the gravestones. On Easter Sunday morning we make the short walk to the church, which local volunteers have filled with greenery and daffodils, returning along the lane to Home Farm for a traditional lunch of spring lamb, after which there is the annual Easter quiz, hosted by friends who live nearby, that fills the afternoon with celebratory cheers as teams race around the village, in search of chocolate eggs.

The truth is, however, that no particular occasion is required in order for a meal to feel celebratory at this time of year and few things give me greater joy than gathering familiar faces around a table laid with dishes that capture the bright, fresh flavours of spring.

Ham, cheese and leek scones

This is a recipe from Claire Ptak's *The Violet Bakery Cookbook*. It's the cookbook I rely on most often for baking, as her recipes are precise and simple. When leeks are cooked slowly, their flavour becomes sweet and nuanced. Spread a little butter over the scones straight out of the oven and you are in for a treat. You can also freeze the prepared scone dough and bake them when you need them. They will keep for a month in the freezer.

Preparation time: 30 minutes, plus 1 hour 10 minutes soaking and chilling time
Cooking time: 45 minutes
Makes: 12 scones

- 2 leeks
- 25 g / 1 oz (1¾ tablespoons) unsalted butter
- 2 tablespoons olive oil
- 1 teaspoon flaky sea salt
- a good grind of black pepper
- 200 g / 7 oz Parmesan cheese, finely grated
- 450 g / 1 lb (3½ cups plus 1½ tablespoons) plain (all-purpose) flour, plus extra for dusting
- 2 tablespoons baking powder
- 100 g / 3½ oz (7 tablespoons) cold unsalted butter, cut into cubes
- 500 g / 1 lb 2 oz (2 cups) plain yogurt
- 200 g / 7 oz your favourite ham (Parma, Serrano, Bayonne or Yorkshire), cut into bite-size pieces
- 1 teaspoon fine sea salt
- 1 egg, lightly beaten with a little milk or water, for the egg wash

Trim the roots and the tough green stalks and outer layer from the leeks. Cut the leeks in half lengthwise and run under cool water to rinse, peeling back the layers to get inside where the grit is lodged. Slice the leeks crosswise into 4-mm (⅙-inch)-thick slices and drop into a bowl of cold water for about 10 minutes. All the dirt will fall to the bottom. Scoop the leeks out (rather than pouring them out with the water) and place in a colander to drain. Pat dry.

In a heavy frying pan over a medium heat, heat the 25 g / 1 oz (1¾ tablespoons) butter and the oil until the butter starts to foam. Add the leeks, the flaky sea salt and the black pepper and sauté for 10–15 minutes until soft but without colour. When they are cooked, tip them in a bowl and chill in the refrigerator for about 20 minutes (this can be done the day before).

Line a baking pan or other container that can fit in your refrigerator with baking (parchment) paper.

In a medium bowl, weigh out the Parmesan, flour and baking powder and stir to combine. Add the cold butter and cut it into the dry mixture with a pastry cutter or the back of a fork (or use a food processor) until crumbly. Add the yogurt, ham, fine sea salt and cooled leeks. Mix quickly to combine, then pat into a cube and place on a lightly floured surface. Pat the dough into a thick log and cut out triangles from the log — you will have about 12. Place the dough triangles on the lined baking pan or other container and put in the refrigerator to chill until set, about 1 hour.

Preheat the oven to 180°C / 350°F / Gas Mark 4. Line a large baking pan with baking paper, place the chilled scones on it and brush them with the egg wash.

Bake in the oven for 25–30 minutes until golden on top, then serve straight away.

Broad bean crostini

These vibrantly coloured, bite-size toasts make the perfect accompaniment to summer drinks. They are to be eaten with your fingers. I also serve these as a starter or as a light lunch.

—

Preparation time: 15 minutes
Cooking time: 10 minutes
Makes: 4 as a starter (appetizer) or 8–10 as a canapé

- 1 tablespon extra virgin olive oil, plus extra for drizzling
- 1 ciabatta, sliced diagonally 1 cm (½ inch) thick
- 1 clove garlic, halved
- 100 g / 3½ oz (¾ cup) shelled broad (fava) beans
- 100 g / 3½ oz (¾ cup) shelled peas
- handful mint leaves
- lemon juice, to taste
- 100 g / 3½ oz soft ewe's cheese or feta cheese, crumbled
- sea salt and black pepper
- pea shoots, to serve

Preheat the oven to 160°C / 325°F / Gas Mark 3.

Drizzle olive oil over the ciabatta slices and cook on a baking sheet in the oven for about 7 minutes until the bread is dry and crispy. Remove from the oven and rub the garlic over the toasted bread while it is still warm.

Bring a saucepan of salted water to the boil. Add the broad (fava) beans and peas and cook for about 2 minutes until they are just soft. Transfer them to a bowl of iced water to stop the cooking and retain the colour, then drain them. Remove the grey outer shell of the broad beans until you have just the bright green bean.

Put most of the mint leaves into a small bowl, together with half of the broad beans and peas and blend with a stick (immersion) blender until they form a rough paste. Add about a tablespoon of olive oil to loosen the paste, balancing the flavours with lemon juice and seasoning with salt and pepper. Smear the paste over the crostini. Spoon on some whole broad beans and peas, along with some crumbled cheese and tear and add the rest of the mint leaves. Season again, place on a wooden board and scatter over some pea shoots to decorate.

Asparagus, pea and herb frittata with Fresh apple, fennel and feta salad

Delicious eaten either hot or cold, this frittata is perfect for brunch or lunch. The apple salad recipe comes from Prue Leith, who is a neighbour of ours in the Cotswolds — you can see her house across the fields beyond our garden. Like me, Prue comes from South Africa. She has been a key figure in the culinary landscape for as long as I can remember and I have undying admiration for her.

Preparation time: 40 minutes
Cooking time: 30 minutes
Serves: 4

For the frittata:
- 3 tablespoons olive oil
- 4 large onions, thinly sliced
- bunch asparagus, spears trimmed and cut into 2-cm (¾-inch) slices
- 6 eggs
- 2 tablespoons milk
- grated zest of 1 lemon
- 1 tablespoon snipped chives
- 1 tablespoon chopped dill
- 1 tablespoon chopped mint
- 1 teaspoon thyme leaves
- 100 g / 3½ oz (⅔ cup) freshly shelled peas or frozen petits pois
- 200 g / 7 oz feta cheese, crumbled
- sea salt

For the salad:
- 1 tablespoon olive oil
- 6 bacon rashers (slices)
- 75 g / 2¾ oz (½ cup) chopped walnuts
- 2 Granny Smith apples
- 1 small fennel bulb
- 75 g / 2¾ oz (½ cup) green or golden raisins
- small handful coriander (cilantro) leaves, finely chopped
- 175 g / 6 oz block of feta, cut into 4 squares
- sea salt and black pepper

For the salad dressing:
- juice of 1 lemon
- 1 clove garlic, crushed
- 4 tablespoons extra virgin olive oil
- pinch of caster (superfine) sugar

GF

Heat the olive oil in a frying pan (skillet) over a low heat, add the onions with a pinch of salt and fry gently for about 20 minutes until they become translucent and begin to caramelize.

Bring a saucepan of salted water to the boil. Add the asparagus spears and cook for 1–2 minutes until they are almost cooked but still firm. Drain.

Break the eggs into a bowl, add the milk and whisk together well. Add the lemon zest and the chopped herbs. When the onions have caramelized, turn up the heat and pour the egg mixture over them. Add the asparagus and peas, using a spoon to distribute the vegetables evenly and cook for a few minutes until the egg mixture is firm. Preheat the grill (broiler) to high.

Once the frittata begins to brown around the edges, scatter on the crumbled feta and put the pan under the hot grill for 1–2 minutes until the cheese starts to soften and go brown. Serve the frittata directly from the frying pan.

Heat the olive oil in a large, heavy frying pan (skillet) over a high heat. Add the bacon and fry until crisp. Drain on paper towels and cut or scrunch into bite-size pieces. Wipe the pan clean and dry, add the walnuts and cook over a medium heat until just toasted. Remove and set aside.

Core and halve the apples. Cut into thin slices and then into fine matchsticks. Cut the base from the fennel bulb. Use a mandoline or your finest knife skills to cut the fennel into paper-thin slices. Mix the apple and fennel with the raisins, coriander (cilantro) and half the walnuts.

Put the dressing ingredients into a big bowl and whisk until smooth and combined. Pour over the salad and gently toss. Serve it from a large bowl or divide among four plates and top with a square of feta, the pieces of bacon and the remaining walnuts.

Lemon posset with thyme shortbread

In its oldest form, posset was a drink of hot milk, curdled with alcohol or citrus and flavoured with spices. From the sixteenth century, it evolved into a drink made from lemon, cream and sugar, similar to syllabub, but with a lighter set and recognizable as the dessert we call 'posset'. It's very simple to make and delicious served with berries and a piece of shortbread, subtly flavoured with thyme and lemon, to add some crunch (this recipe makes plenty of shortbread, so you'll have some left over).

Preparation time: 20 minutes, plus 3 hours setting time
Cooking time: 15 minutes
Serves: 4

- 400 ml / 14 fl oz (1⅔ cups) double (heavy) cream
- 100 g / 3½ oz (½ cup) caster (superfine) sugar
- grated zest and juice of 1 lemon
- lemon thyme flowers, to decorate
- seasonal fresh berries, to serve

For the thyme shortbread:
(makes about 24 shortbread)

- 55 g / 2 oz (¼ cup) caster (superfine) sugar, plus an extra 2 tablespoons for dusting
- 115 g / 4 oz (1 stick) unsalted butter, softened
- grated zest of 2 lemons
- 2 sprigs lemon thyme, leaves picked and finely chopped
- 170 g / 6 oz (1⅓ cups) plain (all-purpose) flour, plus extra for dusting

First, make the possets. Heat the cream in a small saucepan over a low heat and whisk in the sugar. Simmer gently for 3 minutes. Remove from the heat and allow to cool before whisking in the lemon juice and zest. Divide among 4 glasses or small bowls and chill in the refrigerator for about 3 hours until set.

To make the thyme shortbread, preheat the oven to 150°C / 300°F / Gas Mark 2 and lightly grease a baking sheet.

Put the sugar, butter, lemon zest and 2 teaspoons of the thyme leaves into the bowl of a food processor fitted with the beater attachment and beat for a few minutes until pale and creamy. Scrape the mixture into a large bowl and fold in the flour until it's fully combined and the mixture forms a stiff dough.

Place the dough on a sheet of greaseproof (wax) paper and lay another sheet of greaseproof paper on top. Gently roll out the dough until it is about 3 cm (1¼ inches) thick. Remove the top piece of greaseproof paper and stamp out biscuits (cookies) with a floured 5-cm (2-inch) round cutter. Gather all the dough offcuts and repeat until all the dough is used up. Gently place each biscuit on the greased baking sheet and bake in the centre of the oven for about 10 minutes, or until the biscuits are turning very light brown around the edges.

While they're in the oven, mix the remaining sugar and thyme leaves together.

Transfer the biscuits to a cooling rack and immediately sprinkle with the sugar and thyme mix, while the shortbread is still warm.

Decorate the set possets with lemon thyme flowers and serve with fresh berries and shortbread, storing any leftover shortbread in an airtight container for another day.

VG

1

2

3

1 Ham, cheese and leek scones
Broad bean crostini

2 Asparagus, pea and herb frittata
Fresh apple, fennel and feta salad

3 Lemon posset with thyme
shortbread

Chickpea, feta and orange salad

As a rule, I prefer to use chickpeas (garbanzo beans) cooked from scratch, but when there isn't time, I am perfectly happy to open a jar or a can. Here, I have paired the chickpeas with warm baked feta, beetroot (beets), oranges and fresh herbs. When in season, I like to use blood oranges.

Preparation time: 10 minutes
Cooking time: 30–40 minutes
Serves: 2

- 3 small beetroot (beets), trimmed
- 350 g / 12 oz feta
- 2 sprigs thyme, leaves stripped
- olive oil, for drizzling
- 200 g / 7 oz (1¼ cups) drained and rinsed canned chickpeas (garbanzo beans)
- small handful mint or flat-leaf parsley, leaves chopped
- 2 oranges or blood oranges, peeled and sliced into rings
- sea salt and black pepper

For the dressing:
- 2 tablespoons balsamic vinegar
- 1 teaspoon freshly squeezed orange juice
- 2 shallots, very finely chopped
- 1 teaspoon English mustard
- 1 teaspoon honey
- 60 ml / 2 fl oz (¼ cup) extra virgin olive oil

Cook the unpeeled beetroot (beets) in a saucepan of boiling water for 30–40 minutes until tender. Drain, leave to cool a little, then peel off the skin (it should come away easily if you rub it with your fingers) and cut the beetroot into wedges.

In the meantime, preheat the oven to 180°C / 350°F / Gas Mark 4. Place the whole piece of feta in a small ovenproof baking dish, add the thyme and drizzle with olive oil. Roast the feta in the oven for 15 minutes until it is soft.

In a bowl, combine all the dressing ingredients. Add the chickpeas (garbanzo beans) and season to taste with sea salt and pepper. Spoon the chickpeas and their dressing onto two plates and sprinkle with the herbs. Add the sliced oranges and beetroot wedges, followed by the roasted feta, still warm from the oven, and serve.

GF

Tomato, anchovy and herb salad

I use either quinoa, spelt or giant (pearl) couscous for this quick, easy and comforting salad. Adding the oil and vinegar to the cooked grains while they are still warm allows them to absorb more of the dressing, which then melds with the flavours of tomato and anchovy. You can use whichever herbs you like.

Preparation time: 15 minutes
Cooking time: 10 minutes
Serves: 4

- 25 red and yellow cherry tomatoes, halved
- 225 g / 8 oz (about 1 cup) freshly cooked grains, such as spelt, quinoa or giant (pearl) couscous
- 100 ml / 3½ fl oz (⅓ cup plus 1 tablespoon) extra virgin olive oil
- 2 tablespoons red wine vinegar
- ½ cucumber, chopped into small chunks
- 6 canned anchovy fillets (the best quality you can find), torn into pieces
- grated zest and juice of ½ lemon
- handful dill fronds, coarsely chopped
- handful basil leaves, coarsely chopped
- handful mint leaves, coarsely chopped
- handful flat-leaf parsley, coarsely chopped
- sea salt and black pepper

Preheat the oven to 160°C / 325°F / Gas Mark 3. Place the tomatoes on a baking sheet and roast for about 10 minutes until they begin to soften. Remove from the oven and leave to cool.

Put the cooked grains into a bowl while they are still warm, add the olive oil and red wine vinegar and season well with salt and pepper. When the dressed grains have cooled, add the cooled tomatoes, the cucumbers, anchovies and lemon zest and juice. Add the herbs, stir to mix and serve.

Raw tuna with ginger dressing

I was given this recipe by the Notting Hill Fish Shop. As the fish is sliced and eaten raw, it is important to use the very best and freshest tuna loin you can find. The punchy character of the dressing highlights rather than overwhelms the delicate texture and flavour of the fish — the secret is to chop the aromatics with a knife rather than using a food processor. I also make this salad with raw salmon or mackerel. I like to serve it with a fresh green salad.

Preparation time: 20 minutes, plus 10 minutes freezing time
Serves: 4

- 300–400 g / 11–14 oz very fresh tuna fillet, washed and bones and skin removed
- watercress, to serve

For the dressing:
- 1 tablespoon finely chopped garlic
- 5-cm / 2-inch piece of fresh ginger, peeled and finely shredded (to yield 2 tablespoons)
- 2 shallots, finely shredded (to yield 3 tablespoons)
- 50 ml / 1¾ fl oz (3½ tablespoons) lemon juice
- 150 ml / 5 fl oz (⅔ cup) Japanese soy sauce
- 200 ml / 7 fl oz (¾ cup plus 1 tablespoon) sunflower oil

Heat your griddle (grill) pan to a high heat and quickly sear the tuna on all sides until griddle marks appear. Remove from the griddle and, when cooled, place the tuna in the freezer for 10 minutes so it firms up a little. Place 4 serving plates in the refrigerator.

Meanwhile, make the dressing. Mix the garlic, ginger and shallots with the lemon juice, soy sauce and sunflower oil in a bowl, but do not emulsify them.

Remove the tuna from the freezer and slice it thinly across the grain. Lay the slices on very cold plates. Spoon over the dressing, surround the tuna with some watercress and serve.

GF

Spring vegetable stew

This is an Italian dish called Vignole, which comes from Umbria and is based around young vegetables lightly stewed in herbs. It is a real celebration of spring. The sliced pancetta or prosciutto provides flavour but can be omitted if a fully vegetarian dish is preferred. You can be flexible with the ingredients, adding or subtracting vegetables or fresh herbs according to what is to hand, but do keep the artichokes and broad (fava) beans. Serve with a spoonful of wild garlic pesto, if you like, and some bread.

Preparation time: 20 minutes
Cooking time: 25 minutes
Serves: 4

- 6 small artichokes
- 150 g / 5 oz (1 cup) freshly shelled broad (fava) beans
- 4 baby leeks, trimmed and washed
- 4 baby courgettes (zucchini), sliced lengthwise
- bunch asparagus, tough bases trimmed off and each spear cut into 3 pieces
- bunch Swiss chard or spinach, washed and coarsely chopped
- 4 tablespoons olive oil, plus extra for drizzling
- 1 shallot, finely sliced
- 3 cloves garlic, crushed
- 300 ml / 10 fl oz (1¼ cups) vegetable or chicken stock (broth)
- 100 g / 3½ oz (⅔ cup) freshly shelled peas or frozen petits pois
- 4 slices of prosciutto or pancetta, torn into pieces
- small bunch mint, leaves torn
- small bunch flat-leaf parsley, chopped
- handful dill, chopped
- sea salt and black pepper

To serve:
- 4 tablespoons Wild Garlic Pesto (page 068), optional
- good quality crusty bread

Bring a saucepan of salted water to the boil, add the artichokes and cook for 6–10 minutes until the hearts are tender when pierced with a sharp knife, then remove with a slotted spoon. When cool, remove the stalks and outer fibrous leaves to reveal the heart. Remove the chokes with a spoon and cut the remaining tender flesh lengthwise into 4 slices. Set aside.

Blanch the broad (fava) beans in the same saucepan of salted boiling water for about 1 minute. Remove from the water with a slotted spoon and immediately plunge into ice-cold water to stop the cooking and help them retain their vibrancy. Remove the pale skins and set aside.

Blanch the leeks in the same boiling water for 3–4 minutes until just tender, then remove with a slotted spoon. Do the same with the courgettes (zucchini) and asparagus spears until they are just tender. Similarly blanch the chard or spinach for about 30 seconds until just wilted, then drain.

Heat the olive oil in a large sauté pan — one big enough to hold all of the ingredients — over a medium–low heat. Add the shallot and garlic and cook gently for about 2 minutes until soft. Add the stock (broth) and the peas and gently bring to the boil. Add the prosciutto or pancetta pieces and allow to simmer for 2 minutes until the peas are soft and flavoured by the prosciutto. Add all the blanched vegetables and simmer for a few more minutes. Season with salt and pepper. Remove the pan from the heat, add the herbs and drizzle with olive oil. Serve with or without pesto and some bread.

Warm salad of Jersey Royals, asparagus and pancetta

This pretty salad comes from the Daylesford organic farm. We are very lucky to live almost within walking distance of the Daylesford farm shop, which is a constant source of ideas and fabulous organic vegetables. The arrival of Jersey Royals and the start of the asparagus season truly herald the beginning of spring. I think this dish is best eaten warm, but it can also be prepared in advance and served at room temperature.

Preparation time: 5–10 minutes
Cooking time: 15–20 minutes
Serves: 4

- 300 g / 11 oz Jersey Royals, washed, any larger potatoes halved
- 1 teaspoon olive oil
- bunch asparagus, woody ends trimmed
- 8 quail eggs
- 8 thin slices pancetta or Parma ham
- 10 g / ¼ oz fresh dill, coarsely chopped
- 10 g / ¼ oz fresh chives or parsley, coarsely chopped
- sea salt

For the dressing:

- 4 tablespoons garlic mayonnaise
- 2 tablespoons organic yogurt
- 1 tablespoon lemon juice
- generous twist of black pepper

GF

Preheat the oven to 180°C / 350°F / Gas Mark 4.

Bring a pan of salted water to the boil, add the Jersey Royals and simmer for 15–20 minutes until just soft. Drain, run under cold water and set aside.

Meanwhile, heat a griddle (grill) pan until smoking hot. Using your hands, rub the oil and a generous pinch of salt over the asparagus and transfer the spears to the hot griddle. Cook for 4–5 minutes until some lovely char marks begin to appear, then turn the spears and continue to cook them until just softened. Remove from the heat and set aside.

Before preparing the quail eggs, have a bowl of iced water at the ready. Bring a small pan of water to a gentle simmer and gently add the eggs. Cook for 2½ minutes before removing from the pan and immediately plunging them into the iced water. Allow to cool before peeling and cutting each egg in half lengthwise — hopefully revealing a rich, runny yolk.

Put the pancetta or ham into a baking pan, then into the oven for 4–8 minutes until dark and crispy. Break into shards and set aside.

Make your dressing by combining everything in a bowl and mixing thoroughly. Stir half the chopped herbs through the dressing and set aside the remainder.

Toss the coated potatoes in half of the dressing and arrange in a bowl or on a platter. Lay the asparagus, quail eggs, pancetta and the leftover herbs onto the potatoes, before drizzling over the remaining dressing.

Nettle risotto

This recipe is based on the nettle risotto I tasted at Skye Gyngell's wonderful restaurant, Spring. Who would have guessed that this most vicious weed could make such a bright and tasty dish? Make sure to forage the nettles in early spring when the leaves are young and tender. Pick away from roadsides and wear gloves and use scissors to avoid being stung. Nettles can also be made into a highly nutritious soup.

—

Preparation time: 20 minutes
Cooking time: 20–25 minutes
Serves: 4

- 1.5 kg / 3¼ lb nettles, washed with care in 2–3 changes of cold water
- 2.5 litres / 84½ fl oz (10½ cups) vegetable or chicken stock (broth)
- 100 g / 3½ oz (7 tablespoons) unsalted butter, half of it cold and cubed
- 2 shallots, finely chopped
- 400 g / 14 oz (2 cups plus 2 tablespoons) carnaroli risotto rice
- 125 ml / 4¼ fl oz (½ cup) dry white wine
- 90 g / 3¼ oz Parmesan cheese, grated, plus extra to serve
- sea salt and black pepper
- Wild Garlic Pesto (page 068), to serve

Bring a large saucepan of water to the boil, add the nettles and blanch for 30 seconds. Drain but retain a little of the cooking water. Refresh in iced water to stop them cooking and retain their vibrant colour, then drain again and process in a food processor or blender with a little cooking water until smooth. Set aside.

Bring the stock (broth) to the boil in a saucepan, reduce the heat and maintain at a simmer.

Meanwhile, melt half the butter in a heavy sauté pan (keep the cubed butter for finishing the risotto). Add the chopped shallots and cook gently for about 5 minutes, or until softened but not browned. Add the rice and stir until the grains are coated in the butter. Pour in the wine and let it reduce right down. Start to add the warm stock, a ladle or two at a time, stirring gently as the stock is absorbed by the rice. Continue stirring and adding stock for about 15 minutes, then stir in the blended nettles. Keep adding the stock for a few more minutes until the rice is cooked — try a little bit, it should be firm to the bite.

Remove the pan from the heat, cover and leave for a minute, remove the lid and stir in the cubed, cold butter and grated cheese. Season to taste and serve straight away with a small bowl of pesto and another of extra grated Parmesan.

Roast chicken with herbs, lemon and za'atar

Roast chicken is a classic for a reason. It is the ultimate simple dish, which everyone seems to love and is a staple in my household. Not only does it fill the house with the most mouthwatering smells, but the bones can be used afterwards to prepare stock (broth) for soups and risottos. This version has the added flavours of preserved lemon, butter, garlic, herbs and za'atar — a Middle Eastern blend of dried herbs and spices — and I like to serve it with rice, lentils and crisp fried onions to absorb all of the juices.

—

Preparation time: 10 minutes, plus resting time
Cooking time: 1 hour 20 minutes
Serves: 4–6

- 75 g / 2¾ oz (5 tablespoons) unsalted butter, softened
- 4 cloves garlic
- 1 tablespoon finely chopped chives
- 1 tablespoon finely chopped parsley
- 1 tablespoon finely chopped thyme
- 3 preserved lemons, coarsely chopped
- grated zest and juice of ½ lemon
- 1 large free-range chicken (about 1.5 kg / 3¼ lb), at room temperature
- 1 tablespoon za'atar
- sea salt and black pepper

Preheat the oven to 190°C / 375°F / Gas Mark 5.

Put the butter, garlic, herbs, preserved lemon and lemon zest and juice into a small bowl and, using a stick (immersion) blender, blend to make a paste. Using your hands and the back of a dessert or soup spoon, gently and carefully loosen the skin from the breasts of the chicken and spread some of the butter paste evenly under the skin on each breast, smearing the remainder all over the outside of the chicken.

Put the chicken into a roasting pan, sprinkle with the za'atar and season with a generous sprinkling of salt and pepper. Roast in the oven for about 1 hour 20 minutes, basting it frequently with the roasting juices until the skin is golden and the juices run clear when you pierce the thickest part of a thigh with a sharp knife or skewer. Remove from the oven and leave to rest for 15–20 minutes covered loosely with aluminium foil, then serve, along with the roasting juices from the pan.

GF

Seared scallops with pancetta, tomatoes and butter beans

The smoky saltiness of pancetta is a classic foil for the sweetness of scallops. Take care not to overcook the scallops, or they will lose their delicate texture and become rubbery – they should be firm, but still slightly soft to the touch, and the flesh should be opaque, with just a hint of translucence at the very centre.

Preparation time: 20 minutes
Cooking time: 15 minutes
Serves: 4

- 2 large ripe tomatoes, quartered
- 300 g / 11 oz red and yellow cherry tomatoes, halved
- 2–4 tablespoons olive oil, plus extra for drizzling
- small handful fresh oregano leaves, chopped
- 8 slices pancetta
- 1 clove garlic, crushed
- pinch of dried chilli (hot pepper) flakes
- 6 good-quality canned anchovy fillets, chopped
- 1 × 400-g / 14-oz can butter (lima) beans (or cannellini or flageolet beans), drained and rinsed
- 16 scallops, trimmed (roe removed, if preferred)
- large handful salad leaves (greens), such as watercress or rocket (arugula)
- sea salt and black pepper

For the dressing:
- 2 tablespoons lemon juice
- 5 tablespoons extra virgin olive oil

GF

Preheat the oven to 200°C / 400°F / Gas Mark 6.

Pack the tomatoes tightly, skin side down, in a small roasting pan, season generously with salt and pepper, drizzle with olive oil and scatter over the oregano. Roast in the oven for about 15 minutes. Roast the slices of pancetta in a separate roasting pan in the oven for about 10 minutes until crispy.

Meanwhile heat 1–2 tablespoons olive oil in a frying pan (skillet) over a medium heat, add the garlic, chilli (hot pepper) flakes and anchovies and fry for a minute, then add the drained beans and about 30 ml / 1 fl oz (1¾ tablespoons) of water. Bring to a simmer, then remove from the heat and mash to a coarse purée. If the purée is too thick, add more water. Add 1–2 tablespoons olive oil and season with salt and pepper.

Heat a griddle (grill) pan or frying pan (skillet) over a medium heat until hot. Season the scallops, add them to the pan and sear with a touch of olive oil for about 2 minutes until they start to caramelize. Turn and cook on the other side in the same way.

Put some smashed bean purée on each plate and scatter over the roasted tomatoes, salad leaves (greens), crisp pancetta and seared scallops. Whisk the olive oil and lemon juice together and season with salt and pepper, then drizzle over the scallops and serve.

Teriyaki tofu

When it's just the two of us, we find ourselves eating less and less meat. Being naturally bland, tofu is a wonderful vehicle for other flavours, which here include the heat of ginger and raw chilli (chile), the saltiness of soy and the freshness of spring onions (scallions). I particularly like the contrast of the crisp outer shell of the baked tofu with the soft creaminess inside. You can serve it with some steamed broccoli, if you like.

Preparation time: 10 minutes, plus 1 hour 30 minutes draining and marinating time
Cooking time: 30 minutes
Serves: 2

- 300 g / 11 oz extra-firm block tofu
- 2 tablespoons cornflour (cornstarch)
- 3 tablespoons vegetable oil
- 5 spring onions (scallions), trimmed and thinly sliced diagonally
- 1 red chilli (chile), finely chopped
- 1 tablespoon white sesame seeds, toasted
- 1 tablespoon black sesame seeds
- cooked rice, to serve

For the marinade:
- 3-cm (1¼-inch) piece fresh ginger, peeled and finely grated
- 2 cloves garlic, crushed
- ½ tablespoon soft light brown sugar
- 50 ml / 1¾ fl oz (3½ tablespoons) tamari or light soy sauce
- 1 teaspoon sesame oil
- 2 tablespoons mirin or dry sherry

Wrap the tofu in a clean kitchen towel and weigh it down with something heavy to extract the moisture. Leave for 30 minutes, then remove the towel and cut the tofu into 2-cm (¾-inch) cubes.

Combine the marinade ingredients and 60 ml / 2 fl oz (¼ cup) water in a bowl. Put the tofu cubes into the marinade and leave in the refrigerator for 1 hour. Remove the tofu from the marinade with a slotted spoon and toss in the cornflour (cornstarch) until coated on all sides. Heat the vegetable oil in a heavy frying pan (skillet) over a medium–low heat and fry the cubes of tofu on all sides until they become crisp and turn golden. Remove them from the pan with a spatula and leave them to drain on paper towels. Keep warm.

Put the marinade into a small saucepan, bring to the boil, reduce the heat and simmer for a few minutes, stirring until the sauce thickens and reduces by about one third. Stir the crispy tofu cubes into the sauce and garnish with the spring onions (scallions) and chilli (chile). Sprinkle the rice with the sesame seeds and serve.

VE

Linguine with broccoli, Roquefort and walnuts

This is a favourite of mine for a swiftly prepared supper, when I'm too tired to want to fuss over anything more complicated or time-consuming. Particularly during the week, when schedules are busy and liable to change at short notice, it's important to have a few dishes that don't require advance planning. There are always packages of dried pasta in the store cupboard and even when the refrigerator is virtually bare, it is rare for it not to contain tenderstem broccoli (broccolini) and some variety of blue cheese.

Preparation time: 5 minutes
Cooking time: 10 minutes
Serves: 2

- 400 g / 14 oz tenderstem broccoli, (broccolini) washed and stems trimmed
- 250 g / 9 oz linguine
- 250 g / 9 oz Roquefort or any blue cheese, cut into cubes
- 2 handfuls toasted broken walnuts
- sea salt and black pepper
- 2 tablespoons extra virgin olive oil

Bring a large saucepan of salted water to the boil for the pasta and a smaller one for the tenderstem broccoli (broccolini). When the water is boiling, add the broccoli to the smaller pan and cook for 5 minutes until it is soft, but still firm, then drain and set aside. Cook the linguine according to the instructions on the package. Drain it, retaining a small amount of the cooking water, and return the pasta to the saucepan.

Add the Roquefort cheese and retained pasta cooking water to the pasta and stir until it has melted. Add the broccoli and divide between two plates. Sprinkle the walnuts on top of the pasta and add a generous pinch of salt and pepper. Drizzle each serving with the olive oil and serve immediately.

Baked salmon and dill with herb mayonnaise

Fresh green herbs are the perfect accompaniment for the delicate coral pink flesh of salmon, and part baking, part steaming the fish in an aromatic cloud of fennel, lemon and wine or vermouth subtly enhances its flavours. This is a dish that could be prepared outside on a barbecue, but take care not to allow the fish to overcook in the less predictable heat of the coals. Serve it warm with boiled Jersey Royal potatoes and herb mayonnaise.

Preparation time: 20 minutes
Cooking time: 20 minutes
Serves: 4

- 2 × 500-g / 1 lb 2-oz salmon fillets (skin on)
- olive oil, for brushing
- large handful dill, stalks removed and fronds chopped
- 1 fennel bulb, outer leaves removed, tender inner leaves thinly sliced
- 1 lemon, sliced into thin discs
- 30 ml / 1 fl oz (1¾ tablespoons) white wine or vermouth
- handful whole red peppercorns
- sea salt and black pepper

For the herb mayonnaise:

- 2 egg yolks
- 1 clove garlic, crushed
- 1 teaspoon Dijon mustard
- 150 ml / 5 fl oz (⅔ cup) groundnut (peanut) oil
- 50 ml / 1¾ fl oz (3½ tablespoons) extra virgin olive oil
- squeeze of lemon juice
- large handful mixed chopped herbs, such as dill, chervil and snipped chives

Preheat the oven to 200°C / 400°F / Gas Mark 6. Place one salmon fillet on a sheet of aluminium foil, skin side down. Brush with olive oil and season with salt and pepper. Lay the dill fronds on the fish, together with the sliced fennel and the discs of lemon. Sprinkle over the wine or vermouth and place the second salmon fillet on top, skin side up. Season with salt and pepper and scatter the red peppercorns over the top. Wrap the foil loosely around the fish and place in a roasting pan. Bake in the preheated oven for 20 minutes (about 10 minutes per 500 g / 1 lb 2 oz).

While the fish is cooking, make the herb mayonnaise. Use an electric handheld whisk to whisk the egg yolks in a small bowl with the garlic, mustard and some salt and pepper. Pour the groundnut (peanut) oil into a jug (pitcher) and slowly add to the egg mixture, drop by drop, making sure that each addition of oil is thoroughly whisked in before adding the next drop to avoid the mayonnaise splitting. Once all of the groundnut oil has been incorporated, begin adding the olive oil in a steady stream, whisking constantly. Taste and add more seasoning if required, then stir in the lemon juice and herbs.

Remove the fish from the oven and leave it to sit for a while in the foil. Serve warm with the herb mayonnaise on the side.

GF

Butterflied lamb with roasted beetroots and carrots

For me, it is difficult to conceive of an Easter Sunday lunch that does not involve spring lamb. This is a favourite recipe from Skye Gyngell's *Spring* cookbook, which I serve either with Skye's olive and mint sauce or with salsa verde. The well-seasoned meat allows the sweet earthy flavours of the young vegetables to shine through.

Preparation time: 30 minutes, plus 2 hours marinating time
Cooking time: 1 hour 20 minutes
Serves: 8

- a 2-kg / 4½-lb leg of spring lamb, boned and butterflied (ask your butcher to do this)
- 4 cloves garlic, smashed but not peeled
- 6 sprigs thyme
- 100 ml / 3½ fl oz (⅓ cup plus 1 tablespoon) olive oil
- juice of 1 lemon
- bunch beetroot (beets), scrubbed and halved lengthwise
- bunch baby carrots, scrubbed
- 4–6 parsnips, scrubbed and larger ones halved lengthwise
- 5–6 ripe tomatoes
- 3 sprigs rosemary, leaves only, chopped
- sea salt and black pepper

For the olive and mint sauce:
- 100 g / 3½ oz (1 cup) stoned (pitted) good-quality black olives
- bunch mint, leaves only
- 100 ml / 3½ fl oz (⅓ cup plus 1 tablespoon) olive oil
- 2 tablespoons red wine vinegar

Cut the lamb into 6 portions. Mix the garlic, thyme, 4 tablespoons of the olive oil and the lemon juice in a bowl large enough to hold the lamb. Add the lamb and turn to coat well. Cover and leave to marinate for at least 2 hours, turning occasionally.

Meanwhile, prepare the vegetables and sauce. Preheat the oven to 200°C / 400°F / Gas Mark 6. For the sauce, coarsely chop the olives and mint, combine in a bowl and add the olive oil, wine vinegar and a good pinch of salt. Stir well and set aside.

Place the halved beetroot (beets) in a roasting pan, drizzle with 2 tablespoons of the olive oil and season with salt and pepper. Cover the pan tightly with aluminium foil and cook on the middle shelf of the oven for 30 minutes. Add the carrots and parsnips to the pan and toss with the beetroot. Roast, uncovered, for 35 minutes, or until the vegetables are tender when pierced with a sharp knife.

In the meantime, tear the tomatoes in half with your hands and place them in a bowl. Add the chopped rosemary and remaining olive oil, season with salt and pepper and toss to mix. Once the roasted vegetables are cooked, remove from the oven and add the tomatoes. Toss to combine; keep warm.

To cook the lamb, turn the grill to high. Remove the meat from the marinade, pat dry and season well. Grill for a few minutes, turning as necessary to brown well all over, then turn the heat to low and cook for 6 minutes on each side. Remove and set aside in a warm place to rest for 10 minutes.

Slice the lamb and arrange on warm plates with the roasted vegetables. Spoon over some olive and mint sauce to serve.

GF

Piedmontese peppers

The source of this dish is the inimitable Elizabeth David and its confident simplicity and punchy flavours perfectly epitomize her approach to food. I like to use wild garlic pesto. Often found growing alongside bluebells, wild garlic (ramps) is one of the many delights of spring. Forage this seasonal treasure before the plants flower. This recipe makes more pesto than you need for these peppers but it can be kept in a jar in the refrigerator for up to a month. It is a delicious accompaniment to pasta, spring lamb, grilled wild salmon and risotto or swirled through a soup. I have used hazelnuts, but pine nuts or pumpkin seeds work just as well.

Preparation time: 20 minutes
Cooking time: 30 minutes
Serves: 4

- 4 red (bell) peppers, halved and seeded, white ribs removed
- 4 cloves garlic, finely chopped
- 8 anchovies, drained and chopped
- 8 cherry tomatoes, halved
- 8 teaspoons wild garlic pesto
- 200 g / 7 oz mozzarella, torn into pieces
- 8 basil leaves
- sea salt and black pepper
- bread, to serve

For the wild garlic pesto:
- 130 g / 4½ oz wild garlic leaves, (ramps) washed thoroughly
- 50 g / 2 oz (⅓ cup) hazelnuts, toasted and skinned
- 50 g / 2 oz Parmesan cheese, finely grated
- 1 clove garlic
- 130 ml / 4½ fl oz (½ cup) extra virgin olive oil
- squeeze of lemon juice
- sea salt and black pepper

Start by preparing the wild garlic pesto. Put the wild garlic leaves (ramps) into a food processor with the hazelnuts, Parmesan and garlic and pulse until the mixture forms a paste. Drizzle in the olive oil and pulse again until you have a coarse pesto. Taste and season with lemon juice and salt and pepper as necessary. Spoon it into a sterilized 350-g / 12-oz jar and set aside.

Preheat the oven to 200°C / 400°F / Gas Mark 6.

Put the halved red (bell) peppers into an ovenproof dish, skin side down and pack tightly together. Divide the finely chopped garlic cloves among the pepper halves, then divide the chopped anchovies among them, too. Add 2 cherry tomato halves to each pepper half. Season generously with salt and pepper and bake in the oven for about 30 minutes until the peppers are soft.

Remove from the oven and, while the peppers are still hot, add a generous piece of mozzarella to each pepper with a teaspoon of pesto and a basil leaf on the top and serve straight away with bread.

Roast carrots with a creamy tahini dressing

This easy dressing brings Mediterranean flavours to a simple dish of roast carrots. I love the combination of creamy yogurt and tahini, sharpened with lemon and sweetened with honey, together with the freshness of the mint and the bite of chopped, roasted almonds.

Preparation time: 10 minutes
Cooking time: 25 minutes
Serves: 6 as a side dish

- 750 g / 1½ lb carrots, peeled and cut into 2–3-cm (¾–1¼-inch)-thick diagonal slices
- 3 cloves garlic, coarsely chopped
- juice of 1 orange
- 2 tablespoons extra virgin olive oil
- 65 g / 2½ oz (½ cup) almonds, roasted and coarsely chopped
- sea salt and black pepper
- large handful mint leaves, torn, to serve

For the dressing:

- 50 g / 2 oz (3½ tablespoons) tahini
- 350 g / 12 oz (1½ cups) full fat (whole) plain yogurt
- 1 tablespoon lemon juice
- honey, to taste

GF

Preheat the oven to 180°C / 350°F / Gas Mark 4. Put the sliced carrot and garlic into a roasting pan with the orange juice and olive oil and toss with your hands to coat. Season well with salt and pepper. Roast in the oven for about 25 minutes until the carrots are soft and beginning to crisp up.

Meanwhile, whisk together the tahini, yogurt and lemon juice in a bowl, then season to taste with a teaspoon or so of honey and some salt and pepper, then set aside.

Place the carrots on a serving plate and spoon over the dressing. Sprinkle over the chopped almonds and torn mint leaves and serve.

Leeks with breadcrumbs

For this dish, try to find the pencil-thin leeks with crisp white roots that start appearing in farmers' markets in early spring. This dish can be eaten on its own as a starter (appetizer) or as a side dish, which is especially good served with ham.

Preparation time: 10 minutes
Cooking time: 20 minutes
Serves: 4–6 as a side dish or starter (appetizer)

- 20 slender, young leeks, trimmed and rinsed

For the dressing and topping:
- 1 tablespoon white wine vinegar
- 2 tablespoons Dijon mustard
- 5 tablespoons olive oil, plus extra for frying
- 50g / 2 oz (3½ tablespoons) butter
- 120 g / 4 oz (2½ cups) coarse fresh white breadcrumbs
- grated zest of 1 lemon
- handful flat-leaf parsley, chopped
- sea salt and black pepper

Bring a large saucepan of salted water to the boil and add the trimmed leeks. Cook them for 8–10 minutes until they are tender, then drain thoroughly, pat dry with paper towels and lay them in a shallow dish.

Mix the vinegar and mustard in a small bowl or jug (pitcher) with a pinch each of salt and pepper, then whisk in the olive oil. Pour this dressing over the leeks while they are still warm.

Heat the butter in a large frying pan (skillet) with a drizzle of oil over a medium heat. When the butter has melted and is bubbling, add the breadcrumbs. Let the breadcrumbs sizzle, then reduce the heat and brown them over a low heat for 5–10 minutes until golden. Remove from the heat, mix in the lemon zest and chopped parsley, then scatter the mixture over the leeks. Serve while the leeks are still warm.

VG

Lemon and almond cake with pomegranates and pistachios

This gluten free cake is both rich and sharp, with the lemon juice and zest giving it a wonderfully fragrant quality. The combination of the almonds and polenta (cornmeal) creates a lovely moist, crumbly texture, while the bright ruby hues of the pomegranate seeds and the vivid green of the crushed pistachios bring some welcome colour to an overcast day. I like to serve this as a dessert, but a slice also makes an indulgent afternoon treat with a little crème fraiche.

Preparation time: 25 minutes
Cooking time: 30–35 minutes, plus cooling time
Serves: 10–12

- 225 g / 8 oz (2¼ cups) ground almonds (almond meal)
- 110 g / 3¾ oz (¾ cup) polenta (cornmeal)
- ¾ teaspoon baking powder
- pinch of sea salt
- 225 g / 8 oz (2 sticks) unsalted butter, softened, plus extra for greasing
- 190 g / 6½ oz (¾ cup plus 2 tablespoons) caster (superfine) sugar
- 3 eggs
- grated zest of 1½ lemons

For the topping:

- 100 g / 3½ oz (¾ cup plus 1 tablespoon) icing (confectioners') sugar
- juice of 1 lemon
- 100 g / 3½ oz (1 cup) pistachios, crushed
- 100 g / 3½ oz (½ cup plus 2 tablespoons) pomegranate seeds

Preheat the oven to 180°C / 350°F / Gas Mark 4 and grease a 23-cm (9-inch) springform cake pan with butter and line with baking (parchment) paper.

In a large bowl mix together the ground almonds (almond meal), polenta (cornmeal), baking powder and salt. Set aside.

Put the butter and sugar into a large bowl and beat with a wooden spoon until pale yellow. Add two spoonfuls of the ground almond mix, beating all the time. Beat in one of the eggs, then beat in more of the ground almond mix. Continue until you've used all the eggs and ground almond mix, beating continuously. Add the lemon zest, beat again and scrape the mixture into the prepared cake pan. Shake the cake pan or use an offset palette knife (spatula) to level out the mixture.

Bake for 30–35 minutes until the cake starts to shrink away from the edges of the pan. Remove from the oven and leave in the pan to cool, then remove from the pan.

When the cake has cooled, prepare the topping. Sift the icing (confectioners') sugar into a bowl and stir in the lemon juice to make an icing. Smooth this over the top of the cake in a very thin layer and sprinkle the crushed pistachios on top. Just before serving, scatter over the pomegranate seeds. Serve the cake at room temperature.

GF

Walnut praline ice cream

This recipe makes more velvety smooth vanilla ice-cream base than you need for the walnut praline ice cream, but the base is delicious eaten on its own or as an accompaniment to a whole range of fruits, puddings and cakes. It can also be used as the starting point for any number of flavoured ice creams, my personal favourites for summer being blackcurrant ripple and white peach. It is best to make both the vanilla ice-cream base and the praline the day before you are planning to serve this ice cream.

Preparation time: 30 minutes, plus overnight chilling time and churning time
Cooking time: 20–25 minutes
Serves: 6

- 100 g / 3½ oz (¾ cup) walnut pieces, lightly toasted and coarsely chopped

For the vanilla ice-cream base:
- 375 ml / 13 fl oz (1½ cups) milk
- 375 ml / 13 fl oz (1½ cups) double (heavy) cream
- 1 vanilla pod (bean), split in half lengthwise and seeds scraped out
- 150 g / 5 oz (¾ cup) caster (superfine) sugar
- 6 egg yolks

For the praline:
- 100 g / 3½ oz (¾ cup) walnut pieces
- 100 g / 3½ oz (½ cup) caster (superfine) sugar
- pinch of sea salt

VG GF

To make the ice-cream base, put the milk, cream and vanilla seeds into a heavy saucepan and bring to just below simmering point. Reduce the heat to the lowest setting, leave for 5 minutes and then remove from the heat. Allow the vanilla to infuse for 10 minutes.

Put the sugar and egg yolks into a bowl and whisk until thick and pale. Gradually add the milk and cream mixture — it should still be warm — stirring all the while. Transfer to a saucepan and heat it gently over a very low heat, stirring continuously for 10–15 minutes, until the custard is thick enough to coat the back of a spoon. As soon as it is thick enough, remove the pan from the heat and strain the custard through a sieve (fine mesh strainer) into a heatproof bowl. Allow to cool, then cover with clingfilm (plastic wrap) and place in the refrigerator overnight.

On the same day you make the vanilla ice-cream base, also make the praline. Preheat the oven to 160°C / 325°F / Gas Mark 3 and line a baking sheet with baking (parchment) paper. Spread the walnut pieces onto the sheet and toast them in the oven for about 7 minutes or until they begin to brown. Remove from the oven and leave to cool on the baking sheet. Put the caster (superfine) sugar and a pinch of salt into a small heavy saucepan and place over a medium heat. Add 4 tablespoons water and stir to dissolve the sugar and salt. Once the sugar has dissolved, increase the heat to high and stop stirring. When it smells of caramel and has a rich colour, pour it over the walnuts and leave to cool and harden. Break it into small chunks — you can use a rolling pin or sharp knife for this — and store in an airtight container overnight at room temperature.

The next day, remove 500 ml / 17 fl oz (2 cups plus 1 tablespoon) of the ice-cream base from the refrigerator and mix in the chopped walnut pieces before churning in an ice-cream machine according to the manufacturer's instructions until creamy and thick. Add the walnut praline pieces to the ice cream just before you take it out of the machine, while it is still soft, and serve. Any leftover ice cream can be stored in an airtight container in the freezer for a few weeks.

Coconut macaroons

These gluten free sweet treats are very easy to make. They are also a great way to use up egg whites, which seem to be left over in so many recipes.

Preparation time: 5–10 minutes
Cooking time: 15–20 minutes
Makes: about 8 large or 12 small macaroons

- 3 egg whites
- 185 g / 6½ oz (¾ cup plus 1 tablespoon) caster (superfine) sugar
- ¼ teaspoon salt
- 2 teaspoons runny honey
- 150 g / 5 oz (2 cups) unsweetened desiccated (dried) coconut
- ¼ teaspoon vanilla extract

Preheat the oven to 180°C / 350°F / Gas Mark 4 and line a baking sheet with baking (parchment) paper.

Combine the egg whites and sugar in a mixing bowl and beat together thoroughly, then add the remaining ingredients and beat again until everything is well combined and you have a sticky paste.

Scoop 8 small tablespoons or 12 heaped teaspoons of the mixture into mounds onto the lined baking sheet, leaving enough space for the macaroons to expand as they cook. Bake in the oven until they are puffed up and golden. The larger macaroons will need 15–20 minutes, but the smaller ones will take less time to cook. Remove from the oven and allow the macaroons to cool. They will keep for up to a week in an airtight container.

Hazelnut meringue cake

This dessert is deeply nostalgic for me, as it was regularly served by my mother in the seventies, as a Sunday lunch pudding. It is easy to make and has a wonderful nougat flavour and texture to it. The recipe comes from the *Le Cordon Bleu* magazine (issue no. 5, published in 1968) which used to arrive in the post every week in South Africa, where I grew up. I still have part of the collection of these magazines, which are very dog-eared and spattered with food. You can make the meringue the day before and fill it before serving, using whichever soft berries you prefer.

Preparation time: 20 minutes
Cooking time: 30–40 minutes
Serves: 8

- 140 g / 4¾ oz (1 cup) hazelnuts
- 4 egg whites
- 250 g / 9 oz (1¼ cups) caster (superfine) sugar
- a few drops of vanilla extract
- ½ teaspoon white wine vinegar
- butter or a light oil, for greasing

For the filling:
- 300 ml / 10 fl oz (1¼ cups) whipping cream
- 225 g / 8 oz (1¾ cups) raspberries

For the coulis:
- 300 g / 11 oz raspberries or other soft berries
- 1 teaspoon icing (confectioners') sugar

Preheat the oven to 190°C / 375°F / Gas Mark 5. Lightly grease 2 × 20-cm (8-inch) sandwich cake pans and line with greaseproof (wax) paper.

Put the hazelnuts onto a baking sheet and roast in the oven for 5–10 minutes until the skins start to flake away. Remove from the oven and leave to cool, then rub them in clean cloth to remove the skins. Don't worry if all the skin does not come off as a bit of skin adds colour to the meringue. Put the cooled nuts into a plastic bag and crush with a rolling pin. You can use a food processor, but I prefer the nuts not to be too finely ground.

Whisk the egg whites in a clean bowl with a handheld whisk or in a stand mixer fitted with the whisk attachment until stiff. Add the sugar, a tablespoon at a time, with the whisk constantly running, until the mixture forms stiff peaks and all the sugar has been incorporated. Fold in the vanilla extract and vinegar, then fold in the crushed nuts. Divide the mixture between the two prepared pans and level the surface with an offset palette knife (spatula).

Bake in the oven for 30–40 minutes until the top of the meringue is crisp (the inside should be soft and chewy).

Remove from the oven, turn out of the pans and leave to cool before removing the paper.

To make the filling, whisk the cream in a bowl until it is thick. Spread about two thirds of the cream on one of the meringues. Add two thirds of the raspberries. Sandwich the other meringue on top of this. Spread the rest of the cream on the top and sprinkle over the remaining raspberries.

To make the coulis, put the raspberries into a small saucepan with the icing sugar and warm up gently until the fruit begins to release its juices. Pass it through a sieve (fine mesh strainer) and chill in a jug (pitcher) until needed. Serve with the cake (which does not require any additional cream).

GF

Blood orange sorbet with citrus salad

Just when winter seems too barren to bear, blood oranges start arriving in the markets in January and February. I think this is why they are one of my very favourite ingredients, because they bring with them the hope of spring and warmer, longer days. I make this sorbet in February when blood oranges are plentiful and we eat it in early spring. It is a wonderfully palate-cleansing dessert.

Preparation time: 30 minutes, plus freezing time
Serves: 4

For the sorbet:
- 350 ml / 12 fl oz (1½ cups) freshly squeezed blood orange juice
- 125 g / 4½ oz (½ cup plus 2 tablespoons) caster (superfine) sugar
- grated zest of 3 blood oranges
- juice of ½ lemon

For the fruit salad:
- 2 pink grapefruit
- 2 large oranges
- handful mint leaves
- 2 tablespoons pomegranate seeds

Gently heat 100 ml / 3½ fl oz (⅓ cup plus 1 tablespoon) of the blood orange juice in a small saucepan. Add the sugar and stir until the sugar dissolves. Allow the liquid to cool, then add the rest of the orange juice, the zest and the lemon juice. Chill the mixture in the refrigerator for a few hours, then freeze it in an ice-cream maker according to the manufacturer's instructions.

For the salad, peel the grapefruit and oranges, divide into segments and remove all of the white pith. Arrange them on individual plates with the mint leaves and pomegranate seeds. Serve with a scoop of the sorbet.

Although ideally the sorbet will be served as soon as it is made, it will keep in the freezer for up to a month.

Summer

'The sun never knew how great it was until it hit the side of a building.'

Louis Kahn

—

As our feeling of rootedness at Home Farm deepens, so it becomes increasingly difficult to tear ourselves away from the farm for more than a few days at a stretch, particularly in the summer months. Here amongst the quiet spaces of the house, encircled by networks of fields and ancient woodlands, we immerse ourselves in the rhythms of the season and the earth's abundance. Summer at Home Farm is a time for slowing down, for cherishing the longer hours of light and for gathering family and friends around tables and on rugs for picnics under the trees.

Keeping up with deadheading and weeding is a daily task in the herbaceous border, which was planted two years ago and is now filling out.

As the days get hotter, we get up just after sunrise, when there is still a hint of chill to the air, slipping outside to keep on top of tasks like watering, weeding, deadheading, mowing the grass and checking that the fruit in the orchard is setting. There is nothing more exquisite than an English herbaceous border in full bloom in mid June. Although the border at Home Farm is only in its second season, there is always something to bring inside — peonies, alliums, cosmos, lavenders, cornflowers and sweet peas, to mix with armloads of cow parsley collected from the verges — filling the house with fragrance. The roses are in bloom from early summer well into October, with beautiful tuberous dahlias the highlight of a late summer garden.

In the relative cool of the barn kitchen, now is the opportunity to get on with food preparation that can be done in advance. This is also the time to head out to the woods and hedgerows in search of elderflowers to turn into cordial and fritters. After weeks of teasing us with lacy blossoms well out of reach, the frothy white lower-hanging flowers are finally ready for foraging.

In the countryside, where the cadence of the season is experienced more strongly than in the city, there is little point in fighting summer's naturally slower rhythms (and overleaf).

Any early mist swiftly burns away and by mid-morning the views are a shimmering haze. When the noonday sun is at its fiercest, the layers of the landscape banking towards the horizon appear to slump and deform in the heat haze. This is the point in the year when one is keenly aware of the position of the sun at all times of day and the locations of the coolest parts of the house and garden, and John becomes a shadow chaser, camera always in hand, capturing the patterns of light and shadow as they move around the garden and the house.

Home Farm is surrounded by agricultural land and the network of lanes is busy with combine harvesters racing to bring in the crops, tractors cutting and bundling hay for the winter months and calves being moved to fresh fields. Closer to home, the action is focused mainly on and around the pond. Lazy afternoons are spent drifting in the punt. Frogs, newts and carp stir the cold depths of the water. Dragonflies and clouds of smaller insects hum above the surface, occasionally scrutinized by the resident imperious heron. Wild water swimming is done by the brave.

British summers are well known for their unpredictability, but as long as the weather allows it, we try to eat every meal outside, whether in the shade of the pentice or at the massive white marble and stone table we designed, set next to the pond. This table is not something that you can move a little more into the sun or the shade – its considerable weight ensures that it is an equivocally permanent installation. Sometimes we sit on the grass, or in the orchard, or on the steps of the wainhouse.

During the warmest days of summer, there are times when you want to do nothing more strenuous than to sit with something cold to drink, watching the patterns of light and shadow falling across a wall.

These are days when we want to be in the kitchen as little as possible, particularly in proximity to a hot oven. The dishes we enjoy are ones with a few seasonal ingredients, their flavours enhanced with fresh herbs, oils and dressings — courgette (zucchini) flowers stuffed with lemon-scented ricotta, chilled for the lunch table, or an ice-cold gazpacho, served with simple things, such as swiftly seared meat, a plate of pan-fried scallops or a bowl of lightly grilled vegetables. Making summer pudding is an annual ritual, bringing with it the happy, familiar pleasure of lining a bowl with strips of bread, filling it with barely simmered berries, placing a weighted saucer on top and setting it in the refrigerator overnight. A Christmas present of an ice-cream maker has proved a huge success and I love to prepare custard for ice creams that can be chilled, flavoured and churned the following day. Water ices made with a glut of soft fruits are also a favourite, with batches made in the afternoon somehow disappearing by the next morning.

At the local markets and farm shops, the choice is almost overwhelming, with new crops of fruit and vegetables arriving almost daily. The lettuces, mangetouts (snow peas), radishes, sorrel, rocket (arugula), spring onions (scallions), rhubarb and asparagus continue seamlessly from spring into summer and are followed by English peas and broad (fava) beans, young spinach, land cress and basil. Cherries and apricots are the first of summer's stone fruit to ripen. British soft fruits come mainly from orchards in Kent and Sussex — raspberries, redcurrants, gooseberries and blackcurrants. From mid July, if I am lucky and quick, I can collect some coveted mulberries before the birds devour them all (and then leave their crimson droppings all over the white marble table). From France come early strawberries, then white and yellow peaches and nectarines. The short season of summer truffles from France and Spain begins in early July, at the point when home-grown harvests include beetroot (beets), plum tomatoes, young leeks and fennel. We have deep reverence for the earth's awe-inspiring bounty — more so during these months than at any other time of the year.

Preparing cordial from foamy white elderflowers foraged from nearby hedges and woodland is one of the quintessential tasks of summer.

On the last two weekends of June and the first weekend of July, to coincide with the annual sense-assaulting glut of flowers and fruit, nearby Daylesford farm shop opens the 3¼ hectares (8 acres) of its organic kitchen garden for 'pick your own'. Visitors are provided with secateurs (pruners) and baskets and are invited to gather dahlias the size of dinner plates, sweet peas by the armful, young courgettes with the flowers still attached, and tayberries — a cross between a blackberry and raspberry that produces bigger, sweeter fruits than the loganberry — straight from the canes.

In the evenings we like to linger outside for as long as possible, listening for the hoot of the owl and watching the sunsets — their brilliant colours stitching together a vivid new tapestry every day. In the words of Sebastian Flyte in Evelyn Waugh's *Brideshead Revisited* — 'if it could only be like this always — always summer, always alone, the fruit always ripe…'.

Babaganoush and guacamole

Baked aubergine (eggplant) is the principal ingredient of the Mediterranean dish babaganoush. Enriched with olive oil and tahini, and flavoured with garlic, lemon juice and cumin, it is delicious served with flatbread and plenty of sliced vegetables for dipping. Where the babaganoush is smoky and spicy, the avocado-based Mexican dip guacamole offers both coolness and chilli (chile) heat. Both are favourites to take on picnics.

Preparation time: 25 minutes
Cooking time: 30–45 minutes
Makes: about 400 g / 14 oz

For the babaganoush:
- 3 aubergines (eggplants)
- 40 ml / ⅓ fl oz (2¾ tablespoons) olive oil, plus extra for drizzling
- 1 tablespoon cumin seeds, crushed
- 1 tablespoon tahini
- 2 garlic cloves
- juice of 2 lemons
- some pomegranate seeds, for scattering
- sea salt

For the guacamole:
- 4 ripe avocados, halved and stoned (pitted)
- 8 sweet cherry tomatoes, coarsely chopped
- ½ red onion, finely chopped
- 1 teaspoon finely chopped fresh red chilli (chile)
- 2 tablespoons lime juice
- 2 cloves garlic, crushed
- 2 tablespoons chopped coriander (cilantro) leaves, plus extra to serve
- cayenne pepper, to taste
- olive oil, for drizzling

GF

Preheat the oven to 180°C / 350°F / Gas Mark 4.

Slice the aubergines (eggplant) in half lengthwise. Score the flesh deeply in a criss-cross pattern, without cutting through the skin. Drizzle the olive oil over the scored side of the aubergine and scatter over the crushed cumin seeds. Place on a baking sheet, scored side down and bake in the oven for 30–45 minutes until soft. Once cooked, remove from the oven and allow the aubergines to cool before putting them into a bowl with the tahini, garlic, lemon juice, salt and pepper — I leave the aubergine skin on for texture and colour, but you can remove it if preferred, or just leave the skin on half the aubergines and scoop the flesh out of the rest. Blend everything together with a stick (immersion) blender until the mixture has a thick, smooth dipping consistency. Adjust the seasoning, adding more lemon juice if necessary, and transfer to a bowl. Scatter some pomegranate seeds on top and drizzle with some olive oil.

To make the guacamole, scoop the flesh out of the avocados onto a flat plate. Using a fork, mash until smooth. Add the tomatoes, red onion, chilli (chile), lime juice, crushed garlic and coriander (cilantro) leaves. Transfer to a bowl, dust with cayenne pepper, scatter with more coriander and drizzle with olive oil.

Flatbreads

These flatbreads are easy to make and delicious to use to dip into babaganoush and guacamole, as well as to serve alongside a curry or tagine to soak up the juices.

Preparation time: 5 minutes, plus 1 hour resting time
Cooking time: 30 minutes
Makes: about 12 flatbreads

- 350 g / 12 oz (2¾ cups plus 1 tablespoon) self-raising flour, plus extra for dusting
- 1 teaspoon baking powder
- 350 g / 12 oz (1⅓ cups) full-fat (whole) yogurt

For the garlic butter:
- 35 g / 1¼ oz (2½ tablespoons) butter
- 3 small cloves garlic, crushed
- bunch mixed fresh herbs, such as rosemary, parsley, dill, thyme, all finely chopped
- sea salt and black pepper

VG

Combine the flour, baking powder and yogurt in a large mixing bowl, using a palette knife (spatula) initially and then bring it together with your hands until all the flour is incorporated into the dough. Alternatively, process the flour, baking powder and yogurt together in a food processor until it comes together to form a dough.

Lightly dust a clean work counter with flour and tip the dough onto it. Knead gently for about a minute, put it back into the bowl, cover with a plate and leave to sit for 1 hour at room temperature to allow the gluten to develop.

Make the garlic butter by putting the butter in a small saucepan with the garlic and finely chopped herbs. Allow the butter to melt slowly over a low heat, season with salt and pepper and set aside.

Tip the dough out of the bowl onto a lightly floured board or counter. Roll into a sausage shape and slice it into approximately 12 × 2-cm (¾-inch)-thick slices. Flatten each slice with your fingers and then use a lightly flour-dusted rolling pin to roll into irregular shapes 2–3 mm (1⁄16–⅛ inch) thick.

Place a frying pan (skillet) over a high heat. Once it's hot, use a spatula to put a flatbread into the frying pan. Cook for 1–2 minutes on each side, turning it with tongs. The dough will puff up and begin to char. As soon as you remove it from the pan, brush one side with the herby butter. Repeat with the remaining flatbread dough. Warm them up again prior to serving.

Roast chicken and three-rice salad

This recipe is from *Ottolenghi: The Cookbook* and is an all-time family favourite. I sometimes like to adapt the original recipe by adding roasted tomatoes and green beans to the three varieties of rice — basmati, wild and brown — to turn it into a one-dish main course that can be prepared in advance, as is shown on page 102. It is a perfect dish for a picnic as you only need to transport one serving plate and everything is on it.

Preparation time: 20 minutes
Cooking time: 1 hour 10 minutes
Serves: 8

- 1 organic free-range chicken (about 1.5 kg / 3¼ lb)
- 70 ml / 2½ fl oz (⅓ cup) olive oil
- 200 g / 7 oz (1 cup) basmati rice, rinsed
- 50 g / 2 oz (¼ cup) wild rice, rinsed
- 50 g / 2 oz (¼ cup) brown rice, rinsed
- 1 onion, thinly sliced
- 6 spring onions (scallions), thinly sliced
- 4 mild red chillies (chiles), seeded and cut into thin strips
- 50 g / 2 oz coriander (cilantro) chopped
- 20 g / ¾ oz mint leaves, chopped
- 20 shiso leaves, shredded, or rocket (arugula)
- sea salt and black pepper

For the dressing:
- 65 ml / 2 fl oz (¼ cup) lemon juice
- 30 ml / 1 fl oz (1¾ tablespoons) sesame oil
- 30 ml / 1 fl oz (1¾ tablespoons) Thai fish sauce
- 35 ml / 1¼ fl oz (2¼ tablespoons) olive oil

GF

Preheat the oven to 220°C / 425°F / Gas Mark 7.

Rub the chicken with 40 ml / 1⅓ fl oz (2¾ tablespoons) of the olive oil and season liberally with salt and pepper. Place in a roasting pan and put in the oven for 10 minutes.

Reduce the oven temperature to 190°C / 375°F / Gas Mark 5 and continue to roast for 50–60 minutes, basting with the juices occasionally, until the chicken is thoroughly cooked. Remove from the oven and leave to cool to room temperature. Do not get rid of the cooking juices.

While the chicken is roasting, cook the rice. Place the basmati in a saucepan with 400 ml / 14 fl oz (1⅔ cups) of water and a pinch of salt. Bring to the boil, then reduce the heat to minimum, cover and simmer for 20 minutes. Remove from the heat and leave, covered, for 10 minutes. Uncover and leave to cool completely.

Place the wild and brown rice in a saucepan and pour in enough cold water to cover the rice by at least 3 times its volume. Bring to the boil and simmer gently, uncovered, for 40–45 minutes, until the rice is tender but still retains a little firmness. If the water runs low, top up with extra boiling water. Drain through a sieve and run under plenty of cold water to stop the cooking. Leave there to drain.

Carve the meat from the chicken or simply tear it off in largish chunks. Put it in a bowl large enough to hold the whole salad. In a separate bowl, whisk all the dressing ingredients together with the cooking juices from the chicken. Pour the dressing over the chicken and set aside.

Heat the remaining oil in a pan, add the onion and a pinch of salt and fry over a medium heat until golden. Remove from the heat and leave to cool.

Add the 3 rices, the fried onion and spring onions (scallions), chillies (chiles) and chopped herbs to the chicken. Mix well, then taste and adjust the seasoning.

Gooseberry fool

This dessert is simple to make and indulgent to eat. Green and pink gooseberries begin to ripen at the end of June and have a short season. Almost invariably intensely tart in their raw state, they need to be cooked and sweetened with sugar or honey before they can be enjoyed. Adding elderflower cordial brings out the fruit's inherent floral notes.

—

Preparation time: 20 minutes
Cooking time: 30–40 minutes
Serves: 4–6

- 500 g / 1 lb 2 oz (3⅓ cups) gooseberries, topped and tailed
- 1 tablespoon elderflower cordial
- 1–2 tablespoons caster (superfine) sugar (depending on how sweet you like things)
- 100 ml / 3½ fl oz (⅓ cup plus 1 tablespoon) double (heavy) cream
- 100 g / 3½ oz (⅓ cup plus 1 tablespoon) Greek yogurt
- 1–2 tablespoons icing (confectioners') sugar

For the crumble:
- 75 g / 2¾ oz (5½ tablespoons) butter, plus extra for greasing
- 75 g / 2¾ oz (½ cup plus 1 tablespoon) plain (all-purpose) flour
- 50 g / 2¾ oz (6 tablespoons) golden caster (superfine) sugar
- 25 g / 1 oz (4 tablespoons) ground almonds (almond meal)

Put the gooseberries into a saucepan with 1 tablespoon of water, the elderflower cordial and 1 tablespoon of the sugar and simmer gently until the fruit starts to burst. Remove from the heat and mash the fruit to a smooth pulp with a potato masher. Taste to see if it is sweet enough and add more sugar if needed, while the pulp is still warm. Leave to cool before transfering to a bowl and placing in the refrigerator.

To make the crumble, put the butter into a small saucepan and heat it gently over low heat until it melts and begins to turn brown. Pour into a bowl and allow it to cool.

Preheat the oven to 180°C / 350°F / Gas Mark 4 and grease a baking sheet with butter and line with baking (parchment) paper.

Put the cooled butter into a bowl with the flour and rub together, then stir through the sugar and ground almonds (almond meal). Spread out onto the prepared baking sheet and bake in the oven for 25–30 minutes, stirring occasionally, until golden. Remove from the oven and leave to cool.

Meanwhile, whisk the cream in a small bowl until it has thickened, then fold in the yogurt and icing (confectioners') sugar to taste. Place in the refrigerator until ready to serve.

To assemble the fool, spoon some of the chilled gooseberry pulp into the bottom of a glass — use pretty glasses — to form a base layer. Top this with a layer of the thickened cream and a layer of the crumble. Repeat these layers until the glasses are full with the crumble on the top. Serve straight away.

VG

1

2

1 Guacamole (top left), babaganoush and flatbreads

2 Roast chicken and three-rice salad

3 Gooseberry fool, seasonal fruit and shortbread

3

Panzanella

This Tuscan bread and tomato salad is delicious served with a barbecue or roast chicken, cold ham or even as a stand-alone starter (appetizer). I like to dry the bread in the oven to make it crispy, but you can skip this step and allow the bread to become soggy with the tomato juices. Make this in mid summer, when the tomatoes are at their most sweet and ripe. Anchovies and capers are an acquired taste and this salad works perfectly well without them, if preferred. Sometimes I like to add cucumber.

Preparation time: 10 minutes
Cooking time: 15 minutes
Serves: 6–8

- 150 g / 5 oz stale sourdough bread or ciabatta, crust left on, torn into pieces
- olive oil, for drizzling
- 500 g / 1 lb 2 oz mixed ripe tomatoes (preferably heritage tomatoes, for their varied shapes and colours), coarsely chopped
- 1 red onion, finely chopped
- 6–8 canned anchovy fillets, drained and thinly sliced (optional)
- handful capers, drained and rinsed (optional)
- bunch basil, larger leaves torn
- handful mint, leaves coarsely chopped
- sea salt and black pepper

For the dressing:
- 1 heaped teaspoon Dijon mustard
- 2 tablespoons white or red wine vinegar
- 6 tablespoons extra virgin olive oil

Preheat the oven to 180°C / 350°F / Gas Mark 4. Put the torn bread onto a baking sheet, drizzle with olive oil and bake in the oven for about 15 minutes until dry and crisp.

Put the chopped tomatoes and their juices into a large bowl and season with salt and pepper. Add the red onion and anchovies (if using) to the bowl of tomatoes. Squeeze the capers (if using) to remove any juice and add them to the bowl, too.

Whisk all the dressing ingredients together thoroughly in a bowl or jug (pitcher). Add the baked bread and dressing to the tomatoes and toss with your hands. Scatter over the torn basil and chopped mint, season to taste and serve.

Raw courgette, pecorino and pine nut salad

This very simple, light dish requires minimum preparation and no cooking, bar the brief toasting of the pine nuts. It looks very pretty and easily accommodates additional ingredients, such as mozzarella, Parma ham, peas or broad (fava) beans. Use courgettes (zucchini) when they are at their best — firm and not too big.

Preparation time: 15 minutes
Cooking time: 1–2 minutes
Serves: 4

- 30 g / 1 oz (4 tablespoons) pine nuts
- 2 large green courgettes (zucchini)
- 1 large yellow courgette (zucchini)
- 40 g / 1½ oz pecorino cheese
- handful mint leaves
- 30 ml / 1 fl oz (1¾ tablespoons) extra virgin olive oil
- juice of 1 lemon
- sea salt and black pepper

Toast the pine nuts in a dry frying pan (skillet) over a low heat for 1–2 minutes until they begin to turn golden. Remove from the pan and set aside.

Use a potato peeler or mandoline to slice the courgettes (zucchini) into long, thin strips. Slice the pecorino cheese into thin shavings with the same peeler or mandoline. Put the pecorino and courgettes into a bowl, tear over the mint leaves and drizzle with the extra virgin olive oil and lemon juice. Arrange on individual plates and scatter with the toasted pine nuts. Season with salt and pepper and serve.

GF

Gazpacho

With its abundance of fresh raw ingredients, gazpacho is perfectly characterized by the food writer Lindsey Bareham as 'salad soup'. I have many good memories of eating this chilled soup, heady with the scents and flavours of the late spring and summer, with friends in Andalucia.

Preparation time: 20 minutes, plus chilling time
Serves: 6

- 2 red (bell) peppers, seeded and coarsely chopped
- 1 cucumber, chopped
- 1 kg / 2¼ lb mixed ripe tomatoes, skins removed and flesh coarsely chopped
- 2 cloves garlic, finely chopped
- 2 slices slightly stale sourdough bread, with crusts removed, torn into pieces
- 1 tablespoon sherry vinegar
- sea salt and black pepper

To serve:
- olive oil, for drizzling
- finely chopped cucumber
- finely chopped red (bell) pepper
- edible flowers, to decorate
- rye bread

Put the (bell) peppers, cucumber, tomatoes and garlic into a blender or food processor and blend until smooth, in batches if necessary, depending on the capacity of your machine.

Pass this mixture through a sieve (fine-mesh strainer) into a bowl to remove any bits of skin and seeds. Add the torn pieces of sourdough and set aside to allow the bread to soak up the soup. Add the sherry vinegar, season with salt and pepper, return to the blender or food processor and blend until the soup has a velvety smooth consistency. Transfer to a container and place in the refrigerator until well chilled.

Pour into chilled bowls and drizzle with olive oil. Spoon some finely chopped cucumber and red (bell) pepper over the top, decorate with an edible flower and serve straight away with some rye bread.

VG 

Creamy ricotta-stuffed courgette flowers

There is a tiny window in early summer when these vivid orange flowers are available, still attached to the courgettes (zucchini). They are sublime fried in a light batter until crisp, but they also make a wonderfully elegant dish when served raw with a stuffing of creamy ricotta or soft ewe's cheese, delicately flavoured with lemon. This recipe is from Philip McMullen, with whom we have worked for years and who has tirelessly tested all of the recipes for this book.

Preparation time: 30 minutes, plus chilling time
Cooking time: 15 minutes
Serves: 4 (2 flowers per person)

- 300 g / 11 oz ricotta or soft ewe's cheese
- grated zest of 2 unwaxed lemons
- 2 tablespoons pine nuts, toasted
- 2 tablespoons chopped mint leaves
- 8 small courgettes (zucchini) with flowers attached, gently washed
- 30 g / 1¼ oz (2 tablespoons) butter
- 1 shallot, finely chopped
- 1 clove garlic, crushed
- 100 ml / 3½ fl oz (⅓ cup plus 1 tablespoon) vegetable stock (broth)
- sea salt and black pepper

Mix the cheese, lemon zest, pine nuts and mint in a small bowl. With the flower still attached to the courgettes (zucchini), gently pipe or spoon the stuffing into the heads of the flowers. Close the tips of the petals so that the filling remains in place. Once this is done, cut the flower heads off the courgettes, place on a plate and chill in the refrigerator.

Heat the butter in a frying pan (skillet) over a medium–low heat, add the shallot and garlic and cook for about 3 minutes until soft and translucent. Slice the courgettes and add them to the pan along with the vegetable stock (broth) and sweat gently for 10 minutes until the courgettes are tender. Transfer the courgettes to a bowl and purée with a stick (immersion) blender, season to taste with salt and pepper and chill until ready to serve.

Divide the chilled purée among four plates and place two of the stuffed flowers on top of each, or serve from a large dish.

GF

Ceviche

This zingy starter (appetizer) of raw fish marinated in citrus juices is a pleasure to prepare and a delight to eat, with the heat of chopped chillies balanced by the fragrant vibrancy of coriander (cilantro). As the fish is only lightly cured by the acidity of the lemon and lime, it is critical that it is glisteningly fresh. The addition of sliced ripe avocado makes this a more substantial dish.

Preparation time: 20 minutes
Serves: 4

- 400 g / 14 oz skinless very fresh white fish (sea bass, sea bream, halibut or turbot), cut into thinnish slices
- 4 very fresh scallops, white gristle removed, trimmed of their orange 'skirts' and sliced into rounds
- 2 spring onions (scallions), trimmed and thinly sliced
- juice of 1 lemon
- juice of 1 lime
- 2 red chillies (chiles), seeded and finely chopped
- 1 ripe avocado, peeled, stoned (pitted) and thinly sliced
- 2 tablespoons extra virgin olive oil
- 6 sprigs coriander (cilantro), finely chopped
- handful cut mustard cress
- sea salt and black pepper

GF

Put the sliced fish and prepared scallops into a bowl with the spring onions (scallions), cover with clingfilm (plastic wrap) and place in the refrigerator.

Put the lemon and lime juice into a bowl and add a generous pinch of salt and the chopped chilli (chile). Pour the juice over the fish, toss together and put back in the refrigerator. Let the fish marinate in the refrigerator for 10 minutes, but no more. This should be long enough for the citric acid to 'cook' the fish.

Place a helping of the ceviche on individual plates and drizzle with a little of the citrus juice. Add some slices of avocado to each plate and drizzle with a little extra virgin olive oil. Sprinkle with the finely chopped coriander (cilantro) and mustard cress, add some black pepper and serve.

Goat's cheese and thyme soufflé

This recipe is from one of my favourite London chefs, Sally Clarke. Her restaurant in Kensington Church Street, not too far from where we live, is the one we choose over most others and has been consistently excellent for over 30 years. This soufflé is not made in a traditional soufflé dish but in individual (ovenproof) soup bowls. It is quick and simple to prepare and, as it does not have a traditional roux base, it has the additional benefit of being gluten free.

Preparation time: 10–15 minutes
Cooking time: 8–10 minutes
Serves: 6

- 50 g / 2 oz (3½ tablespoons) unsalted butter, plus extra for greasing
- 200 g / 7 oz Parmesan cheese, finely grated, plus extra for sprinkling
- 6 eggs, separated
- 400 g / 14 oz soft goat's cheese
- 150 ml / 5 fl oz (⅔ cup) double (heavy) cream
- 1 tablespoon chopped thyme leaves, plus a few extra for sprinkling
- sea salt and black pepper

Preheat the oven to 200°C / 400°F / Gas Mark 6. Butter 6 ovenproof bowls and sprinkle with a quarter of the grated Parmesan.

Whisk the egg yolks in a bowl until smooth, add the goat's cheese and whisk again. Stir in the cream and season with the chopped thyme and some salt and pepper. Fold in the remaining Parmesan.

In a separate clean bowl, whisk the egg whites with a pinch of salt until stiff peaks form. Fold the whites carefully but thoroughly into the cheese mix. Divide among the dishes and sprinkle with the extra thyme leaves and a little Parmesan.

Place the bowls on a baking sheet in the oven and bake in the oven for 8–10 minutes until golden and risen. Serve straight away — and don't forget to warn your guests that the bowls are oven-hot.

GF

Tomato, oregano and olive tarts

Reminiscent of the more familiar marjoram and thyme, oregano has an earthy, citrusy flavour with notes of pine, making it the perfect partner to tomatoes. As the weather gets warmer and the days longer, I could happily eat all three meals outside and these simple but elegant tarts are easily robust enough to take straight from the oven to the garden table. You can use a ready-made puff pastry for this recipe if you prefer. I like to serve these tarts with a green salad.

Preparation time: 30 minutes, plus 25 minutes chilling time
Cooking time: 30–35 minutes
Makes: 4 individual or 1 large tart

For the pastry:
- 140 g / 4¾ oz (1 cup plus 2 tablespoons) plain (all-purpose) flour, plus extra for dusting
- ¼ teaspoon caster (superfine) sugar
- pinch of salt
- 75 g / 2¾ oz (5 tablespoons) cold unsalted butter, cut into small cubes
- 2–3 tablespoons iced water
- 1 egg
- olive oil, for drizzling

For the filling:
- 2 tablespoons extra virgin olive oil
- 6 shallots, thinly sliced
- pinch of salt
- 6 ripe tomatoes, cut into thick slices
- small bunch oregano leaves
- 100 g / 3½ oz (½ cup) green or black olives, stoned (pitted) and halved
- sea salt and black pepper

To serve:
- salad leaves (greens)

VG

First, make the pastry dough. Put the flour, sugar and salt into a food processor. Add the cold butter and pulse a few times to mix, being careful not to over work it – there should still be lumps. Gradually add enough iced water to bring everything together. Shape into a flat disc, wrap in clingfilm (plastic wrap) and refrigerate for 25 minutes.

To make the filling, heat the extra virgin olive oil in a heavy frying pan (skillet) over a low heat, add the shallots and salt and sauté for 10 minutes until they are soft and translucent and beginning to caramelize. Remove from the heat and set aside.

Preheat the oven to 180°C / 350°F / Gas Mark 4 and line a baking sheet with baking (parchment) paper.

Divide the chilled pastry dough into quarters. Roll each quarter first into a ball, then roll out on a lightly floured work counter to a thickness of about 3 mm (⅛ inch). You can roll them into rounds or squares. (Alternatively, roll the pastry out to make 1 large tart.) Lift the rolled dough onto the prepared sheet and sprinkle with a little flour. Spoon the shallots and tomatoes on top, leaving a border of 2.5 cm (1 inch). Sprinkle over half the oregano and add the olives. In a small bowl, lightly beat the egg. Fold the rim of pastry up over the filling and brush the pastry with the beaten egg.

Whether you are making 1 large tart or 4 individual ones, bake them in the oven for 30–35 minutes until golden. Drizzle over some olive oil, season with salt and pepper, sprinkle over the remaining oregano and serve with salad leaves (greens).

Grilled peach, mozzarella and rocket salad

I could eat this simple salad every day. The recipe calls for only a handful of ingredients and minimal cooking. Grilling the peaches enhances their flavour and releases some of their juices, which helps enrich the dressing.

Preparation time: 5 minutes
Cooking time: 10 minutes
Serves: 4

- 4 ripe peaches, halved and stoned (pitted)
- 130 g / 4½ oz rocket (arugula) or watercress
- 2 large balls buffalo mozzarella, drained
- sea salt and black pepper

For the dressing:
- 3 tablespoons extra virgin olive oil
- juice of 1 lemon

Heat a griddle (grill) pan over a high heat. Lay the peach halves, cut-side down, on the hot griddle pan and grill them for about 5 minutes until the flesh is clearly marked with griddle lines.

Place a handful of rocket (arugula) on each plate. Tear the buffalo mozzarella into pieces and place next to the rocket along with the grilled peaches.

Mix the olive oil and lemon juice together, drizzle over the salad, season well and serve immediately.

GF

Stir-fried sea bass with soy, ginger and vegetables

The mild, sweet flavour and meaty texture of sea bass makes it a good choice for people who struggle with the stronger smell and taste of some other types of fish. In recent years, sea bass has been heavily fished, but stocks are slowly recovering, with line-caught being the more sustainable option. I like to use the gleaming white fillets in this dish, which is inspired by Alastair Little's recipe in his cookbook *Keep It Simple*, based on a dish he tasted at Poons restaurant in London.

Preparation time: 10 minutes
Cooking time: 9–10 minutes
Serves: 4

- 4 medium sea bass fillets
- 6 spring onions (scallions), trimmed
- 200 g / 7 oz (6⅔ cups) spinach, washed
- 2 small carrots, shaved into strips
- 2 tablespoons light soy sauce
- juice of 1 lemon
- 3-cm (1¼-inch) piece of fresh ginger, peeled and finely grated
- 2 cloves garlic, thinly sliced
- 2 tablespoons plain (all-purpose) flour
- 1 tablespoon olive oil
- 1 red chilli (chile), seeded and thinly sliced
- sea salt
- cooked wholegrain or plain rice, to serve

Slice the fish, at an angle, into 2-cm (¾-inch)-thick pieces and leave in the refrigerator while you prepare the vegetables.

Heat a griddle (grill) pan over a high heat, then chargrill the spring onions (scallions) for 4–5 minutes and set aside. Bring a large saucepan of salted water to the boil. Add the spinach and blanch for 45 seconds, then remove with a slotted spoon and drain on paper towels. Blanch the carrot strips in the same boiling water for 1 minute to soften them slightly, then drain and set aside.

To make a sauce, combine the soy sauce, lemon juice, grated ginger and sliced garlic in a small bowl and set aside.

Put the flour on a plate and coat the fish pieces in it. Heat the oil in a heavy wok or frying pan (skillet) over a medium heat, add the fish and fry for about 1 minute. Do this in two pans if it does not fit into one. Turn the fish pieces over and add the blanched vegetables and sauce. Cook for another minute. Add the sliced chilli (chile) and serve with rice.

GF

Gruyère and cherry tomato quiche

I find myself making this quiche repeatedly through the weeks of summer for lunches and picnics. Mixing a little finely grated Gruyère cheese into the pastry dough adds a lovely savouriness and intensifies the flavour of the dish as a whole.

Preparation time: 15 minutes, plus 1 hour 30 minutes chilling time for the pastry
Cooking time: 1 hour 55 minutes
Serves: 6–8

For the pastry:
- 200 g / 7 oz (1⅔ cups) plain (all-purpose) flour, plus extra for dusting
- pinch of salt
- 100 g / 3½ oz (7 tablespoons) unsalted butter, well chilled, cut into small cubes
- 60 g / 2 oz Gruyère cheese, finely grated
- 1 egg, separated
- a little iced water

For the filling:
- 550 g / 1 lb 2 oz (1½ cups) cherry tomatoes, halved
- 1 tablespoon olive oil
- 1 tablespoon basil leaves, torn
- 2 eggs
- 150 ml / 5 fl oz (⅔ cup) single (light) cream
- 150 ml / 5 fl oz (⅔ cup) milk
- 90 g / 3¼ oz Gruyère cheese finely grated
- sea salt and black pepper

To serve:
- salad leaves (greens)

To make the pastry dough, tip the flour and salt into a food processor and add the chilled butter. Pulse until the mixture has the consistency of fine breadcrumbs. Add the Gruyère cheese and egg yolk and process again, then, with the motor still running, trickle in just enough iced water (a teaspoon or two) to bring the dough together in lumps. Transfer the dough to a large bowl and gather it into a ball with your hands. Wrap the pastry in clingfilm (plastic wrap) and leave to rest in the refrigerator for at least 1 hour.

Unwrap the chilled pastry dough, knead it until it is pliable, then roll it out thinly on a lightly floured work counter into a large circle 26 cm (10¼ inches) in diameter. Carefully lift the pastry onto the rolling pin and drape it over a loose-bottomed 23 x 4-cm (9 x 1½-inch) tart pan. Press into the sides of the pan and trim the top using a knife. Chill the pastry case in the refrigerator for 30 minutes.

Preheat the oven to 190°C / 375°F / Gas Mark 5.

Remove the pastry case (shell) from the refrigerator and prick the base with a fork. Line the pastry case with greaseproof (wax) paper, fill with baking beans (pie weights) and bake 'blind' on the middle shelf of the oven for 15 minutes. Remove the paper and beans, brush the inside of the case with the egg white, then bake in the oven for another 10 minutes until the pastry is golden brown and crisp. Remove from the oven, transfer to a cooling rack and leave to cool completely.

Reduce the oven temperature to 140°C / 275°F / Gas Mark 1. Lay the halved cherry tomatoes cut side up on a baking sheet. Drizzle with the olive oil and scatter over the torn basil leaves. Season with salt and pepper and roast for about 1 hour. Remove from the oven and set aside. Increase the oven to 190°C / 375°F / Gas Mark 5.

To make the filling, gently whisk the eggs in a bowl, then whisk in the cream and milk. Season with salt and pepper and stir in the grated cheese. Pour the mixture into the cooled pastry case and arrange the roasted cherry tomatoes evenly over the top, cut side up. Bake in the oven for 25–30 minutes until set and golden. Remove from the oven and leave the tart to cool in the pan before serving with salad leaves (greens).

Alphonso mango, avocado and beef salad

Early summer brings many delights to eat, none greater than the much-revered Alphonso mango from India, where it is known as the king of mangoes. Small, sweet and buttery in texture, I like to use them in this salad, where they are combined with tender fillet (tenderloin) steak and avocado. If you are unable to source these mangoes, choose another with a bright orange flesh. This is a great party dish that also works well using grilled chicken breast in place of the beef.

Preparation time: 10 minutes, plus 1 hour marinating time
Cooking time: 15–20 minutes
Serves: 8

For the marinade:
- 2 small cloves garlic, crushed
- 2 tablespoons sesame oil
- 2 teaspoons dark soy sauce
- 1 teaspoon light muscovado sugar
- 1 teaspoon grated fresh ginger
- pinch of black pepper

For the salad:
- 800 g / 1¾ lb fillet (tenderloin) steak in one piece, trimmed
- 3 Alphonso mangoes
- 2 ripe avocados
- 3–4 handfuls watercress or salad leaves (greens)

For the dressing:
- 2 tablespoons Thai fish sauce
- 1 tablespoon toasted sesame oil
- juice of 1 lime
- 1 tablespoon light soy sauce
- 1 teaspoon light muscovado sugar
- 1 chilli (chile), halved, seeded and finely chopped
- 2 small cloves garlic, crushed
- sea salt, to taste

GF

Whisk together all the ingredients for the marinade in a large bowl. Add the steak and coat it in the marinade, using your hands to rub it in. Leave to marinate for about 1 hour.

Preheat the oven to 200°C / 400°F / Gas Mark 6.

Heat a griddle (grill) pan over a high heat. Place the marinated steak in the hot pan and sear for a minute on each side, turning it over so that it has griddle marks on both sides. Put it in a roasting pan and transfer to the oven for 5 minutes, then reduce the heat to 180°C / 350°F / Gas Mark 4 and cook for another 10 minutes. If you want your meat more well done, leave it in the oven for longer. Remove from the oven, transfer to a plate and leave it to rest for 15 minutes before slicing it thinly.

Peel the mangoes, cut the flesh from the stones (pits) and slice into large wedges. Peel, stone and thickly slice the avocados.

Whisk together the ingredients for the dressing.

Arrange the salad leaves (greens) on a large platter. Place the steak, mango and avocado on top, drizzle over the dressing along with any juices from the rested steak and serve immediately.

Lemon pasta

This recipe, inspired by the River Café's lemon spaghetti, is a very simple dish to make and satisfyingly rich and creamy — for a lighter version, omit the cream and butter. If I can find them, I like to use Sicilian or Amalfi lemons and I think this recipe works particularly well with orecchiette (the 'little ears' from Puglia in southern Italy), but the dish will accommodate whatever form of pasta you have in the cupboard.

Preparation time: 5 minutes
Cooking time: 10 minutes
Serves: 6

- 400 g / 14 oz pasta
- 100 ml / 3½ fl oz (⅓ cup plus 1 tablespoon) double (heavy) cream
- 25 g / 1 oz (1¾ tablespoons) butter
- juice of 3 lemons and grated zest of 2 lemons
- 150 ml / 5 fl oz (⅔ cup) olive oil
- 120 g / 4 oz Parmesan cheese, grated
- 2 handfuls basil, leaves freshly torn
- sea salt and black pepper

Cook the pasta in a large saucepan in a generous amount of salted boiling water, according to the instructions on the package.

While the pasta is cooking, pour the cream into a large saucepan, place over a medium heat and let it bubble and reduce for a few minutes, then add the butter. Take off the heat and slowly whisk in the lemon juice and olive oil. Drain the pasta when it is ready and add it to the sauce, followed by the Parmesan. Stir everything together. Tip onto a large serving plate with the torn basil and lemon zest scattered on top. Season well with salt and pepper and serve straight away.

Aubergine Parmigiana

This robust dish is a family favourite, served either alongside lamb, or on its own as a main course with wholegrain rice. It takes a while to make, as all of the aubergine (eggplant) slices need to be cooked in batches, but on a day when there is no pressure on time, there is an almost meditative pleasure in the repetitive nature of the task. To shorten the process — and reduce the quantity of oil — the cookery writer Jane Grigson suggests parboiling a proportion of the aubergines, which seems to work just as well as when they're all fried and produces a lighter dish. You can make the passata (tomato puree) from scratch, but you can save time by using a good quality shop-bought one. I think that this dish improves if made the day before and warmed up before serving.

Preparation time: 30 minutes, plus 25 minutes draining
Cooking time: 1 hour 25 minutes
Serves: 4

- 1.5 kg / 3¼ lb (about 3 large) aubergines (eggplants)
- fine salt, for salting
- 200 ml / 7 fl oz (¾ cup plus 2 tablespoons) olive oil, plus extra for drizzling
- butter, for greasing
- 800 g / 1¾ lb (3¼ cups) good-quality passata (tomato puree)
- 200 g / 7 oz mozzarella, thinly sliced
- 120 g / 4 oz Parmesan cheese, grated, plus extra to sprinkle
- 65 g / 2½ oz (½ cup plus 2 tablespoons) breadcrumbs
- fine sea salt and black pepper
- salad leaves (greens), to serve

Cut the aubergines (eggplants) lengthwise into 5-mm / ¼-inch-thick slices, sprinkle with salt and put them into a colander. Leave them to drain for 25 minutes at room temperature. Thoroughly rinse the aubergine slices under cold running water to remove the salt, then dry well with paper towels. Pour enough oil into a frying pan (skillet) to coat the bottom generously and set over a high heat. Line a plate with paper towels. Fry the aubergine slices, a few at a time, until golden on both sides, then transfer to the lined plate to soak up any excess oil.

Preheat the oven to 180°C / 350°F / Gas Mark 4 and grease a baking dish with butter. Spoon a little passata (tomato puree) into the prepared baking dish. Top this with a layer each of aubergine slices, mozzarella, grated Parmesan and seasoning, making sure you pack everything in tightly. Keep building up the layers in this way until you run out of aubergine slices, then top with a final layer of passata (you may not use it all). Reserve a little Parmesan for the top.

Put the breadcrumbs, the reserved Parmesan and a drizzle of olive oil into a small bowl and gently mix, then sprinkle over the top layer of passata. Bake the parmigiana in the oven for about 40 minutes until bubbling and the breadcrumb topping is golden. Allow to cool slightly, then serve with salad leaves (greens).

Cherry, broad bean and radish salad

Three of the finest ingredients of summer combine here to make a gloriously vibrant salad, bright with colour and texture. You can adjust the proportion of broad (fava) beans to cherries.

Preparation time: 15 minutes
Cooking time: 2 minutes
Serves: 4

- 350 g / 12 oz (2½ cups) stoned (pitted) and halved cherries
- 60 g / 2¼ oz (½ cup) sliced radishes
- 250 g / 9 oz (1¾ cups) shelled broad (fava) beans
- thyme flowers, to serve

For the dressing:
- 4 tablespoons orange juice
- 4 tablespoons olive oil
- 2 tablespoons chopped dill
- sea salt and black pepper

Put the halved cherries and radishes into a serving bowl.

Bring a saucepan of salted water to the boil, add the broad (fava) beans and cook for 2 minutes until tender but still firm. Drain and plunge into a bowl of iced water to stop the cooking and preserve the vibrant colour of the beans. Drain again and remove the pale outer skins, then add to the cherries and radishes.

Whisk all of the dressing ingredients together, seasoning to taste. Pour the dressing over the salad, toss gently so that the juice from the cherries does not bleed too much over the other ingredients, sprinkle with thyme flowers and serve.

Purple sprouting broccoli with anchovies

Purple sprouting broccoli (broccolini) is one of the first leafy vegetables of the year and its stalks are tender and delicate. In this simple but robustly flavoured recipe, the anchovy sauce with chilli (chile) seasons the broccoli, giving it a salty, spicy kick. This dish is delicious on its own as a warm side dish and is also perfect served over pasta.

Preparation time: 10 minutes
Cooking time: 2–3 minutes
Serves: 4 as a side dish

- 6 canned anchovy fillets in oil, finely chopped
- 1 clove garlic
- juice of ½ lemon
- 50 ml / 1¾ fl oz (3½ tablespoons) extra virgin olive oil
- 500 g / 1 lb 2 oz purple sprouting broccoli (broccolini), trimmed of thick stalks and leaves
- 1 red chilli (chile), seeded and finely chopped
- sea salt and black pepper

Pound the anchovies with the garlic, lemon juice, olive oil and a pinch of black pepper to a thick paste in a mortar with a pestle.

Bring a large saucepan of salted water to the boil and cook the trimmed broccoli for 2–3 minutes until the stalks are firm but tender. Drain the broccoli, transfer to a serving bowl and immediately toss in the anchovy sauce and sprinkle with finely chopped chilli (chile). This dish is nicest served warm.

GF

Strawberry clafoutis with elderflower cream

I love the classic French dish clafoutis — sweet custardy batter, studded with fruit whose flavour has been intensified by the heat of the oven. Combining two of my favourite summer ingredients, this recipe was created especially for this book by Claire Ptak, food writer and owner of the Violet bakery in east London, not too far from where our elder son now lives.

—

Preparation time: 20 minutes
Cooking time: 40–45 minutes
Serves: 6

For the clafoutis:
- 50 g / 2 oz (3½ tablespoons) unsalted butter
- 600 g / 1 lb 5 oz strawberries, hulled and halved
- 70 g / 2¾ oz (½ cup plus 1 tablespoon) plain (all-purpose) flour
- ½ teaspoon ground cinnamon
- pinch of salt
- 150 g / 5 oz (¾ cup) caster (superfine) sugar
- 3 eggs
- 300 ml / 10 fl oz (1¼ cups) milk
- icing (confectioners') sugar, for dusting (optional)

For the elderflower cream:
- 300 ml / 10 fl oz (1¼ cups) double (heavy) cream
- 2 tablespoons elderflower cordial

Preheat the oven to 190°C / 375°F / Gas Mark 5.

Spread 25 g / 1 oz (1¾ tablespoons) of the butter inside a 23-cm (9-inch) oval baking dish. Fill with the hulled and halved strawberries, arranged cut side down in a single layer.

Whisk together the flour, cinnamon, salt and 100 g / 3½ oz (½ cup) of the caster (superfine) sugar. Whisk in the eggs, one by one, followed by the milk, then pour this mixture over the strawberries.

Sprinkle with the remaining 50 g / 2 oz (¼ cup) sugar. Cut the remaining 25 g / 1 oz (1¾ tablespoons) of butter into tiny pieces and scatter on the top.

Bake in the oven for 40–45 minutes until puffed and lightly golden. Remove from the oven and let it cool completely before cutting, sprinkling with icing sugar if desired.

While you let the clafoutis cool, prepare the elderflower cream. Pour the cream into a bowl and stir in the elderflower cordial — don't whip the cream completely, as you want it to be loose. Serve the cream alongside the warm clafoutis.

VG

Elderflower and raspberry jelly

These gently floral elderflower jellies, studded with raspberries, beautifully capture the flavours of early summer. The quantity of gelatine in this recipe produces a soft set, ensuring quivering rather than bouncy jellies, while the suspended bubbles of prosecco feel naturally celebratory.

Preparation time: 20 minutes, plus 3–4 hours setting time
Cooking time: 2–3 minutes
Serves: 4

- 300 g / 11 oz raspberries
- juice of 1 lemon
- 1 tablespoon caster (superfine) sugar
- 4 leaves (sheets) gelatine
- 200 ml / 7 fl oz (3/4 cup plus 2 tablespoons) elderflower cordial
- 100 ml / 3 1/2 fl oz (1/3 cup plus 1 tablespoon) prosecco
- elderflower heads, thoroughly cleaned and blossoms picked, to decorate

Arrange about 50 g / 2 oz of the raspberries in four 150 ml / 5 fl oz (2/3 cup) moulds or darioles. Slice the remaining raspberries in half, place in a small bowl, add the lemon juice and caster (superfine) sugar and leave in the refrigerator to macerate.

Soften the gelatine in a bowl of cold water for 10 minutes.

Put the elderflower cordial and half of the prosecco into a saucepan and heat until just simmering, then remove from heat. Remove the softened gelatine leaves from the bowl and squeeze out any excess water. Add the gelatine to the saucepan and stir until dissolved. Remove from the heat and add the remaining prosecco. Stir gently to keep the bubbles of the prosecco. Carefully pour into the moulds and put the moulds into the refrigerator for 3–4 hours to set.

Turn the moulds out onto individual plates and serve with a spoonful of the macerated raspberries and some elderflower blossoms for decoration.

GF

Rye, cranberry and chocolate cookies

This recipe was given to me by Moko Hirayama who, with her husband, is the owner of the charming, tiny restaurant Mokonuts in the 11th arrondissement of Paris. The menu in the restaurant is always thoughtful and exquisite and the restaurant is always packed. The addition of poppy seeds, cranberries and rye flour make these cookies very special.

—

Preparation time: 15 minutes, plus overnight chilling time
Cooking time: 20 minutes
Makes: about 15 cookies

- 130 g / 4½ oz (1⅓ cups) medium rye flour
- 85 g / 3 oz (⅔ cup) plain (all-purpose) flour
- 1 teaspoon baking powder
- ¾ teaspoon fine sea salt
- ½ teaspoon bicarbonate of soda (baking soda)
- 140 g / 4¾ oz (1¼ sticks) softened unsalted butter, cubed
- 100 g / 3½ oz (½ cup) caster (superfine) sugar
- 100 g / 3½ oz (½ cup) light brown sugar
- 1 egg
- 80 g / 3 oz (⅔ cup) plump dried cranberries
- 50 g / 2 oz (⅓ cup) poppy seeds
- 110 g / 3¾ oz dark (bittersweet) chocolate, cut into small chunks
- sea salt flakes, for sprinkling

Mix together the rye flour, plain (all-purpose) flour, baking powder, fine salt and bicarbonate of soda (baking soda) in a medium bowl and set aside.

Put the butter and both sugars into a large bowl and beat using an electric mixer on medium speed for about 3 minutes or in a stand mixer fitted with a paddle attachment until pale and creamy. Add the egg and beat for another 2 minutes, then add the mixed dry ingredients, followed by the cranberries, poppy seeds and chocolate. Stir with a wooden spoon until everything is incorporated.

Divide the dough into about 15 pieces and roll into balls between your palms. Wrap each ball in clingfilm (plastic wrap) and refrigerate overnight – you can freeze the dough balls at this stage if you want to bake the cookies later.

Preheat the oven to 180°C / 350°C / Gas Mark 4 and line a baking sheet with greaseproof (wax) paper. Put half the cookies onto the baking sheet set 5 cm / 2 inches apart to allow for spreading. Lightly sprinkle with crushed sea salt and bake for 10 minutes on the middle shelf of the oven. Keep the rest of the dough balls in the refrigerator.

Remove from the oven, lightly tap each cookie with a metal spatula and allow to rest on the baking sheet for a few minutes. Transfer to a cooling rack, and bake the remaining cookies. Serve while the cookies are still warm and the chocolate is soft.

VG

Summer pudding

I make this a number of times every summer, adjusting the mix of berries and currants to reflect whatever is most bountiful – whether I'm picking them myself or buying them. It is a simple and satisfying dish to prepare, with the advantage that virtually everything is done the day before, while honouring the essential fresh, bright flavours of the fruit.

Preparation time: 40 minutes, plus overnight chilling time
Cooking time: 5 minutes
Serves: 8–10

- 7–8 slices slightly stale white bread, with the crusts removed
- 300 g / 11 oz (2⅔ cups) blackcurrants
- 200 g / 7 oz (1⅓ cups) blackberries
- 200 g / 7 oz (1⅔ cups) raspberries
- 100 g / 3½ oz (⅔ cup) strawberries
- 100 g / 3½ oz (¾ cup) redcurrants
- 250 g / 9 oz (1¼ cups) caster (superfine) sugar
- grated zest and juice of 1 lemon
- crème fraîche or yogurt, to serve

Line a 1-litre / 34-fl oz (4½-cup) pudding basin or deep heatproof bowl with clingfilm (plastic wrap) and then with about 5 slices of the white bread, overlapping the pieces and pressing them into the sides of the bowl so that the bread forms a tight inner bowl.

Rinse all the berries and put them into a medium saucepan with the sugar and lemon zest and juice. Let them stew gently over a low heat until they begin to release their juices, then remove from the heat and leave to cool and allow the flavours to develop.

Once cool, use a slotted spoon to transfer the fruit into the bread-lined basin, filling it to the brim. Spoon over the remaining juices, reserving about a cupful. Cover the bowl with the remaining bread and some clingfilm. Put a saucer on the top to weigh it and place in the refrigerator overnight.

To serve, fold back the clingfilm and carefully invert the pudding onto a deep plate. Brush any pale areas of the bread with the reserved juice. Serve with crème fraîche or yogurt.

VG

Apricot frangipane tart

In this tart fresh apricots are baked in a bed of lemon-scented frangipane, a sweet almond filling that perfectly complements the sharpness of the stone fruit.

Preparation time: 30 minutes, plus minimum 1 hour 30 minutes chilling time
Cooking time: 1 hour 25 minutes
Serves: 6–8

For the pastry:
- 200 g / 7 oz (1⅔ cups) plain (all-purpose) flour, plus extra for dusting
- 100 g / 3½ oz (7 tablespoons) cold unsalted butter
- 2 tablespoons icing (confectioners') sugar
- pinch of salt
- 2 egg yolks
- ice-cold water to bring the pastry together if needed

For the filling:
- 200 g / 7 oz (1¾ sticks) softened unsalted butter
- 180 g / 6 oz (¾ cup plus 2 tablespoons) caster (superfine) sugar
- 200 g / 7 oz (2 cups) ground almonds (almond meal)
- grated zest and juice of 1 lemon
- 1 egg
- 8 ripe apricots, halved and stoned (pitted)

To make the pastry dough, put the flour and butter into a food processor. Pulse until the mixture resembles coarse breadcrumbs. Add the sugar, salt and egg yolks and pulse until the mixture just leaves the sides of the bowl. Alternatively, to make the pastry dough by hand, put the flour and butter in a bowl and rub the butter gently and swiftly into the flour with your fingertips until the mixture resembles coarse breadcrumbs, then add the sugar, salt and egg yolks and rub it through your fingers lightly until it comes together to form a dough. Shape into a ball, wrap in clingfilm (plastic wrap), flatten it slightly and refrigerate for at least 1 hour.

Remove the pastry dough from the refrigerator and let it soften a little, then roll it out on a lightly floured surface until large enough to line a 23-cm (9-inch) shallow loose-bottomed tart pan. Press the pastry dough evenly into the sides and base of the pan and return to the refrigerator for 30 minutes.

Preheat the oven to 180°C / 350°F / Gas Mark 4. Put a sheet of greaseproof (wax) paper over the chilled tart case (shell), fill with baking beans (pie weights) and bake 'blind' for 20 minutes. Remove the beans and the greaseproof paper and return the pastry case (shell) to the oven briefly to allow the pastry to turn golden. Remove from the oven and allow the pastry to cool completely.

To make the frangipane, cream the butter and sugar in a food processor or in the bowl of a stand mixer fitted with the beater attachment until pale and fluffy in texture. Add the ground almonds (almond meal) and pulse to combine. Gradually add the grated lemon zest and juice, pulsing again. Remove from the processor or mixer and use a wooden spoon to stir in the egg.

Spread a layer of about half the frangipane over the pastry case, then place the apricots, cut side up, on top. Fill the spaces between the apricots with more of the frangipane. Bake the tart in the oven for 1 hour, or until the frangipane is set. Remove from the oven and leave to cool in the tart pan. Serve at room temperature.

VG

Autumn

'I don't divide architecture, landscape and gardening; to me they are one.'

Luis Barragán

—

After the brilliance of summer, autumn (fall) is a quieter season. As the length of the days dwindles we become accustomed to spending more of our time in the absence of natural light. It is a time for gathering wild and cultivated harvests and a time for gathering thoughts. The character of the landscape changes. Everywhere there is a sea of yellows, reds, oranges, browns, rusts, purples and blacks. As the leaves fall — gradually, over a period of weeks, or torn off in a few frenzied hours by the fury of a single storm — the structure of the trees and the underlying contours of the countryside begin to emerge.

In the northern hemisphere, autumn (fall) is bookended by the late September equinox and the winter solstice in December and is a period of profound change in the garden and the landscape surrounding Home Farm.

On many mornings at Home Farm the view is misty across the rolling hills and the tracery of fields and hedges, but on a crisp autumn morning, when the air is clear, the landscape can be exhilaratingly austere. Different things catch the eye — a bloom of oxidation on a section of steel, the ghost traces of formwork on a concrete wall and the textures of a trod path through a field of recently cut wheat.

Setting out for a walk in summer is pretty straightforward, but now scarves, hats, raincoats and boots need to be found. The cold air is energizing and there is much pleasure in arriving back tired and covered in mud, to light a fire and linger over a cup of tea and a slice of cake, enjoying the feeling of cosiness. As the weeks pass, we tend to spend less time in the barn and more in the smaller spaces of the farmhouse. Previously expansive vistas narrow and become more intimate. Curtains are drawn, playing cards and board games come out and we watch films through the long evenings.

As the season advances, more time is spent indoors. Fires and stoves are lit and while the barn (overleaf) continues to serve as a key gathering space, there is also a gradual drift towards the more intimate spaces of the farmhouse, the garden room and the library.

It is not yet time to retreat entirely indoors, however. There are endless tasks to do in the garden, with cutting back and pruning in the borders. Tulip, daffodil, hyacinth and crocus bulbs are planted. Tender herbs are moved inside in pots, windfalls are collected and wood chopped and stacked for the fires. In the orchard the pears and apples are harvested and sent to a co-operative to be made into cider. Meantime the leaf-raking seems to go on for weeks. The Home Farm punt is covered up and stored. Soon, when the beehives have been installed, we will need to help the colonies survive through to spring. For as long as possible, whenever the weather permits, we eke out the chances to eat at the outdoor table, with the help of rugs and thermal clothing.

Each season brings its own excitements and autumn is no exception. The hedgerows and woodlands become a plentiful larder (pantry) and nothing gives us more pleasure than to rummage in them during our walks. Blackberries are everywhere. On our return from the walks, fingers stained a brilliant purple, we put our foraged haul to use immediately, making blackberry and apple crumbles (crisps), compotes and jellies. We also make sloe gins from the blueish-black sloes, pricking the berries before infusing (steeping) them for a year in a mixture of spirit (liquor) and sugar, so that there is a bottle to open for Christmas each year.

Tempting as it may be to seek the comfort of a blazing fire, there are many outdoor tasks to be accomplished in the dwindling hours of daylight.

It is at this point in the turning year that our attention naturally begins to focus on the family gatherings of the festive season, now only a matter of weeks away. Even though contemporary life, with its freezers and year-round access to produce from across the world, makes it unnecessary to lay things down for the winter months, there is still something reassuring in the act of making preserves and filling the larder (pantry) with stores, driven by some deep-rooted instinct to accomplish tasks and feel purposeful. Air-freighted goods may make it feasible to maintain a perpetual summer table, but at Home Farm recipes begin to revolve around autumn staples, like apples and squash, but also to take account of less obvious seasonal highlights, like crab and chicory.

For me one of the welcome signs of autumn is the appearance, from early October to mid-November, of wet walnuts — a creamy treat with a distinctive flavour, delicious broken over a crisp salad or eaten with cheese. The ancient woodlands and hedgerows surrounding Home Farm are also filled with cobnuts — sweet, husky nuts of the hazelnut family that must be foraged before the squirrels get to them. From September the local shops and farmers' markets start to fill with pumpkins, turnips, parsnips, squashes and swedes (rutabagas), yellow and purple beans, red and green chard, beetroot (beets) of various colours, finger aubergines (eggplant), corn on the cob, later varieties of tomato, marjoram, purple figs and flowering mint. October and November see the coming of the British crops of wild mushrooms. Ceps (porcini) and brown and yellow chanterelles mushrooms arrive from France. From Italy we have radicchio, celeriac (celery root) and white truffles. Orchard fruit at Home Farm includes Falstaff, Bramley, Gala and Cox's apples as well as Conference and Comice pears, quinces, plums and damsons.

There is pleasure in wrapping up warmly to cook over an open fire with friends, watching conversations turn to patterns of mist in the cold, damp air.

It is not only the palette of fresh ingredients that shifts, along with our appetite for different flavour profiles and textures, but also the way we want to cook. At this time of year I am more than happy to spend time indoors, in proximity to the heat of the hob (stove) and oven. Autumn's gently bolstering, nourishing dishes benefit from quietly steeping, resting and maturing. This is a time for slow cooking — for soups, stews and casseroles. Whether meat or plant-based, menus usually involve some element of slow braising, roasting or baking and there is something very comforting about a stockpot simmering gently on the hob, filling the house with soothing smells, as the days become shorter.

Bonfire Night is an annual commemoration in the UK, in the first week of November. Wood for the fire has been accumulating for weeks, heaped up for maximum drama. When finally lit, the flames shoot high into the night sky, projecting a show of dancing light across the honey-coloured stone walls of Home Farm. We huddle together, sipping mulled wine, watching the excitement on the children's faces as the dry timber snaps and crackles, savouring the experience of being out in the crisp air, the landscape sharp then black, while a batch of lamb skewers grills over hot coals.

Cheese straws

For me there is no better accompaniment to pre-dinner drinks than the salty, crumbly savouriness of a good cheese straw. I prefer them made with short rather than puff pastry and without any fancy twisting. This is a perfect recipe for using up any old pieces of Cheddar, as the drier the cheese the better from both taste and texture perspectives. Combining Parmesan with the Cheddar intensifies the cheesiness of the straws, while the cayenne pepper and English mustard powder add a touch of heat.

Preparation time: 20 minutes, plus 25 minutes chilling time
Cooking time: 15–20 minutes
Makes: about 20 straws

- 375 g / 13 oz (3 cups) plain (all-purpose) flour
- pinch of fine salt
- 225 g / 8 oz (2 sticks) cold butter, diced
- 100 g / 3½ oz mature Cheddar cheese, finely grated
- 100 g / 3½ oz Parmesan cheese, finely grated
- 2 egg yolks
- ¼ teaspoon English mustard powder
- ¼ teaspoon cayenne pepper
- 3 tablespoons iced water

Sift the flour and salt into a bowl and add the butter. Using your fingers, rub the butter into the salt and flour until there are no lumps and it resembles coarse breadcrumbs. Add the Cheddar, Parmesan, egg yolks, mustard powder and cayenne and stir to mix. Add the iced water and mix to form a dough. Shape into a ball, wrap in clingfilm (plastic wrap) and leave to rest in the refrigerator for 25 minutes.

Preheat the oven to 180°C / 350°F / Gas Mark 4 and line a baking sheet with baking (parchment) paper.

Unwrap the dough and roll it out on a work counter lightly dusted with flour into a square 4 mm (⅙ inch) thick. Cut the dough into 1-cm (½-inch)-thick strips, lift and place on the lined baking sheet and bake for 15–20 minutes until crisp and golden. Remove from the oven and leave to cool slightly on the sheet. Serve warm.

Bagna càuda with crudités

Bagna càuda translates literally as 'hot bath'. It is a deliciously unctuous and flavourful sauce for dressing grilled vegetables or for serving as a dip with raw vegetables. The dish originated in the Piedmont area of northwest Italy and was typically prepared in the colder months after the harvest was in, when the varieties of vegetables that traditionally accompany it were coming into season. If I'm using the sauce as a dip, I put a tealight under the bowl to keep it warm.

Preparation time: 20 minutes
Makes: 350 ml / 12 fl oz (1½ cups)

- 3 shallots, finely chopped
- 5 cloves garlic, crushed
- 8–10 anchovy fillets (preferably Ortiz)
- 50 ml / 1¾ fl oz (3½ tablespoons) red wine vinegar
- 1 teaspoon lemon juice
- 150 ml / 5 fl oz (⅔ cup) extra virgin olive oil
- 90 ml / 3 fl oz (6 tablespoons) double (heavy) cream
- raw or grilled mixed seasonal vegetables, to serve

Blend all the ingredients except the cream in a blender. Add the cream and stir until smooth. Serve either poured over grilled vegetables or in a bowl as a dip for raw vegetables. I like to serve it with as many brightly coloured vegetables as are available: carrots, courgettes (zucchini), radishes, endive, celery, cucumber, asparagus and even some cooked small potatoes.

GF

Lamb kebabs with pear and hazelnut coleslaw

Regardless of whether you are wrapped up outside or inside in the warm, these pitta breads filled with lamb are best eaten with your fingers. They work really well with this coleslaw, which is based on a recipe from Skye Gyngell's excellent cookbook *Spring*. I like to add grated carrots and sliced fennel.

Preparation time: 30 minutes, plus overnight marinating
Cooking time: 5 minutes
Serves: 6

For the lamb:

- 6 cloves garlic, finely chopped
- 180 ml / 6 fl oz (¾ cup) olive oil
- 1½ generous tablespoons za'atar
- 1½ generous tablespoons tamari
- ½ teaspoon dried chilli flakes
- grated zest and juice of 1 lemon
- half a deboned leg of lamb, cut into 3-cm (1¼-inch) cubes
- sea salt and black pepper

For the coleslaw:

- ¼ red cabbage, cored and shredded
- ¼ white (green) cabbage, cored and shredded
- 1 fennel bulb, thinly sliced
- 3 carrots, grated
- 3 firm, ripe pears
- 120 g / 4 oz (¾ cup) blanched hazelnuts, toasted and chopped
- chopped flat-leaf parsley, to serve (optional)
- sea salt and black pepper

For the coleslaw dressing:

- ½ tablespoon Dijon mustard
- 1 teaspoon honey
- 1 egg yolk
- 1 tablespoon cider (apple) vinegar
- 180 ml / 6 fl oz (¾ cup) olive oil
- 4 tablespoons buttermilk
- sea salt and black pepper

To serve:

- 6 pitta breads
- 1 cos (romaine) lettuce, shredded
- 6 tomatoes, sliced
- juice of 1 lemon
- 10 spring onions (scallions), sliced
- chopped coriander (cilantro)

To make the lamb skewers, mix together all the lamb ingredients in a small bowl except for the meat, salt and pepper. Put 8 pieces of the lamb onto each of 6 metal skewers, place in a shallow flat dish and season with salt and pepper. Pour the marinade over the skewers and marinate for several hours or preferably overnight.

The next day, prepare the coleslaw. Combine the shredded red and white (green) cabbage in a bowl with the fennel and carrot. Halve, core and thinly slice the pears. Add them to the cabbage, fennel and carrot, toss lightly, season with salt and pepper and add the chopped hazelnuts.

To make the coleslaw dressing, put the mustard, honey, egg yolk and vinegar into a small bowl. Season with a little salt and pepper and stir vigorously to combine, then slowly whisk in the olive oil, increasing the flow as it homogenizes with the egg yolk mixture. Continue until all the oil is incorporated, stir in the buttermilk and taste to adjust the seasoning as necessary. Pour the dressing over the salad and mix together gently using your fingertips. Set aside and sprinkle with parsley, if using, when ready to serve.

Heat your barbecue or preheat your grill (broiler) to its maximum setting. Cook the skewers on the barbecue, or on an aluminium-foil lined rack under the grill, for 5 minutes, turning them often.

Warm the pitta bread on the barbecue grill (or in a warm oven). Split them open and fill with the lettuce and tomatoes. Take the meat off the skewers and add it to the pitta bread, sprinkle with lemon juice, add the spring onions (scallions) and coriander (cilantro) and serve with the coleslaw.

Rustic apple tart

Because the patterned arrangement of the fruit is integral to this recipe, it is important to choose the right apples. You need a variety that will hold its shape and not disintegrate during cooking. I use Cox's Orange Pippins, which I am lucky enough to be able to pick from a tree in the Home Farm orchard; Granny Smith or Braeburn will also work.

Preparation time: 20 minutes, plus 30 minutes chilling time
Cooking time: 1 hour
Serves: 8

For the pastry:
- 140 g / 4¾ oz (1 cup plus 2 tablespoons) plain (all-purpose) flour, plus extra for dusting
- pinch of salt
- 2 tablespoons icing (confectioners') sugar
- 85 g / 3¼ oz (6 tablespoons) cold unsalted butter, cut into 1-cm (½-inch) cubes
- 1 egg, beaten
- 1 teaspoon lemon juice
- 2 tablespoons iced water

For the filling:
- 6 crisp eating (dessert) apples
- 50 g / 2 oz (¼ cup) caster (superfine) sugar
- 1 cinnamon stick
- pinch of salt
- 25 g / 1 oz (1¾ tablespoons) unsalted butter, cut into small pieces
- 2 tablespoons apricot jam (preserves), warmed and pressed through a sieve (fine-mesh strainer), for glazing

To serve:
- vanilla ice cream or crème fraîche

VG

Begin by making the pastry dough. Put the flour, salt and sugar into a bowl and mix, then rub in the cold butter gently and swiftly with your fingertips, until the mixture resembles coarse breadcrumbs. The butter does not need to be finely mixed in as the lumps will actually make the pastry flakier. Push the mixture to the sides of the bowl to form a well in the middle.

In a small bowl, mix the egg with the lemon juice and iced water, then pour the liquid into the well in the flour mix, a little at a time, rubbing it through your fingers lightly until it comes together as a dough (you may not need all of the liquid). Shape into a flat disc, wrap in clingfilm (plastic wrap) and refrigerate for 25 minutes. When the pastry has rested, remove it from the refrigerator and let it soften while you prepare the filling.

Peel and core half of the apples, cut them into chunks and put them into a small saucepan with 2 tablespoons of water, 1 tablespoon of the sugar and the cinnamon stick. Stew the apples over a medium–low heat for 10–15 minutes or until they are soft and have formed a lumpy purée. Strain off any excess juice to avoid soggy pastry and remove the cinnamon stick.

Slice the rest of the apples into 4-mm (⅛-inch)-thick wedges, leaving the skins on. Put them into a bowl, add the salt and all but 1 tablespoon of the sugar and mix briefly to combine.

Preheat the oven to 180°C / 350°F / Gas Mark 4 and line a baking sheet with baking (parchment) paper.

Unwrap and roll out the pastry dough on a lightly floured surface to a circle about 30 cm (12 inches) in diameter. Gently lift the dough onto the lined baking sheet. Spoon the apple purée onto the middle of the pastry, leaving a border of at least 5 cm (2 inches) all the way around. Arrange the apple wedges over the apple purée. Fold the edge of the pastry over the apples and gently press in the edges. Sprinkle over the remaining sugar and scatter with small pieces of the butter.

Bake in the oven for 40–45 minutes, or until the pastry is golden. Remove from the oven, brush the apricot glaze over the tart and serve warm with vanilla ice cream or crème fraîche.

2

1

3

1 Bagna càuda with crudités
Cheese straws

2 Lamb kebabs with pear and hazelnut coleslaw

3 Rustic apple tart

Grilled polenta and mushrooms

Polenta is what cornmeal becomes when it is cooked. It comes in a range of textures from fine to coarse and in two colours – yellow and the delicately flavoured white variety more common in the Veneto region of northern Italy. In its traditional forms, polenta requires slow cooking and assiduous stirring, but there is also a quick-cooking version that I find gives a perfectly good result for this recipe. The polenta here is cooked then allowed to cool and set, before being sliced, grilled and loaded with truffle-scented mushrooms.

Preparation time: 15 minutes, plus setting time
Cooking time: 25 minutes–1 hour, depending on the type of polenta
Serves: 2

- 475 ml / 16 fl oz (2 cups) vegetable stock (broth)
- 75 g / 2¾ oz (½ cup) quick-cook or traditional polenta (cornmeal)
- 60 g / 2 oz Parmesan cheese, grated
- 45 g / 1¾ oz (3 tablespoons) butter
- 1 teaspoon finely chopped rosemary
- 1 tablespoon finely chopped parsley
- 3 tablespoons olive oil, plus extra for brushing
- 2 shallots, finely diced
- 1 large clove garlic, finely diced
- 350 g / 12 oz mixed mushrooms, coarsely chopped
- 1½ tablespoons chopped tarragon
- 1 tablespoon chopped thyme
- drizzle of truffle oil (optional)
- handful snipped chives, to serve
- sea salt and black pepper

Pour the stock into a saucepan, bring to the boil over a medium heat and gradually stir in the polenta (cornmeal). Reduce the heat to low and stir gently with a wooden spoon for about 5 minutes (if using quick-cook polenta) or up to 45 minutes (for traditional polenta) until it has thickened a little and leaves the sides of the pan. Stir in the Parmesan, 35 g / 1¼ oz (2½ tablespoons) of the butter, the rosemary and parsley and season to taste. Spread the polenta into a heatproof dish and leave to set.

Heat the olive oil and the remaining butter in a large frying pan (skillet) over a medium heat. Add the shallots and garlic and sauté for 5 minutes until translucent. Add the mushrooms and fry for a few minutes until they are just cooked, then turn off the heat and add the tarragon, thyme, truffle oil and some salt and pepper. Keep warm.

When the polenta has set, remove it from the dish, cut it into pieces, brush it with olive oil and grill it on a hot griddle (grill) pan for about 4 minutes on each side. Remove from the pan, top with the mushrooms and their juices and put in the oven for a minute to heat through. Serve sprinkled with snipped chives.

GF

Roast onion, fig and blue cheese salad

The appeal of this dish lies in the combination of sweet, sour, bitter and salty. The natural sweetness of the red onions is enhanced by roasting them with a little olive oil, balsamic vinegar and honey, to encourage caramelization. Cooking the figs briefly until the juices run deepens their innate sweetness and helps intensify the flavour of any fruits that are less than ideally ripe. Salty cheese serves as the foil for all of this jammy stickiness.

Preparation time: 10 minutes
Cooking time: 25 minutes
Serves: 4

- 3 or 4 small red onions or shallots, peeled and cut into wedges
- 2 tablespoons good quality sherry vinegar
- 1 teaspoon honey
- 45 ml / 1½ fl oz (3 tablespoons) extra virgin olive oil, plus extra for drizzling
- 8 ripe figs, halved
- 100 g / 3½ oz (¾ cup) walnuts or pecans
- 1 head of radicchio, washed
- generous handful salad leaves (greens)
- 140 g / 5 oz English blue cheese, I like the ones made by Cropwell Bishop
- sea salt and black pepper

For the dressing:
- 40 ml / 1¼ fl oz (2½ tablespoons) extra virgin olive oil
- juice of 1 lime

GF

Preheat the oven to 180°C / 350°F / Gas Mark 4.

Put the onion wedges into a large roasting pan, season well with salt and pepper and toss with half the vinegar, the honey and enough olive oil to coat. Roast in the oven for 25 minutes until soft and slightly charred at the edges.

While the onion wedges are roasting, put the figs, cut side down, into a separate roasting pan. Season with salt and pepper and drizzle with olive oil. Roast in the oven for 10 minutes until softened but still holding their shape.

Remove the figs and onions from the oven and drizzle the figs with the remaining vinegar. Toast the walnuts in a small pan over a low heat for 4–5 minutes until slightly darker in colour. Transfer to a chopping (cutting) board and coarsely chop.

To make the dressing, pour any juice from the fig roasting pan into a small bowl and whisk in the olive oil and lime juice. Season with salt and pepper.

Place the radicchio and salad leaves (greens) on a large serving plate and top with the onions and figs. Scatter over the blue cheese and nuts, drizzle with the dressing and serve.

Butternut squash and pumpkin soup

While butternut squash is readily available throughout the year, pumpkins are mainly seasonal, but together they combine — both in colour and beta-carotene content — to create a rich, hearty, velvet-textured soup. Without herbs or spices to detract from the comforting sweetness of the butternut and pumpkin, the flavour is underpinned by subtle allium notes of onions, garlic and leeks. I like to roast the squash and pumpkin before adding them to the stock as this produces a deeper flavour.

Preparation time: 30 minutes
Cooking time: 1 hour
Serves: 8–10

- 1 kg / 2¼ lb pumpkin, peeled, seeded and diced (about 500 g / 1 lb 2 oz)
- 1 kg / 2¼ lb butternut squash, peeled, seeded and diced (about 500 g / 1 lb 2 oz)
- 90 ml / 3 fl oz (6 tablespoons) olive oil
- 2 tablespoons pumpkin seeds
- 2 large onions, chopped
- 4 cloves garlic, chopped
- 300 kg / 11 oz leeks, trimmed and chopped
- 1 litre / 34 fl oz (4¼ cups) vegetable stock (broth)
- double (heavy) cream, for drizzling
- sea salt and black pepper
- rye fruit bread, to serve

Preheat the oven to 180°C / 350°F / Gas Mark 4. Put the prepared pumpkin and butternut squash into a large roasting pan and season with salt and pepper. Coat them in 60 ml / 2 fl oz (4 tablespoons) olive oil and roast for about 30 minutes until soft and lightly browned. Put the pumpkin seeds on a baking sheet and toast them in the oven for 5 minutes — keep an eye on them to make sure they don't burn.

Meanwhile, heat the remaining olive oil in a large saucepan over a medium–low heat, add the onions and garlic and sauté for about 5 minutes until translucent. Add the leeks and continue to cook for another 20 minutes until the leeks are softened but not browned. Stir in the roasted squash and pumpkin and continue to sauté for 5 minutes, then pour in the stock (broth) and cook for another 30 minutes. Transfer to a blender, blend until smooth and season to taste.

Ladle the soup into bowls, sprinkle with the toasted pumpkin seeds, drizzle with cream and serve with some bread on the side.

VG

Figs, buffalo mozzarella and Parma ham

This recipe is reminiscent of those dishes usually associated with the height of summer, which take moments to assemble and are based on a few components, chosen for their contrasting but complementary colours, textures and flavours. It doesn't involve cooking — I tend to avoid recipes that are fiddly to prepare or that have too many ingredients. Ideally use figs that are at their ripest and eat the salad immediately after preparing, served with this simple olive oil and lemon juice dressing.

Preparation time: 15 minutes
Serves: 6

- 3 balls buffalo mozzarella
- 12 thin slices Parma ham or Serrano ham
- 12 ripe, green or purple figs, washed, tops cut off and fruit quartered
- large handful salad leaves (greens)
- sea salt and black pepper

For the dressing:
- juice of 2 lemons
- 40 ml / 1⅓ fl oz (2¾ tablespoons) extra virgin olive oil

Tear each mozzarella ball into quarters. Lay two slices of Parma ham on each plate, placing the fig quarters and mozzarella on top. Add some salad leaves (greens) and season with salt and pepper.

To make the dressing, mix the lemon juice and olive oil together and season generously. Drizzle the dressing over each plate and serve straight away.

GF

Crevette with samphire and lemon butter sauce

The term 'crevette' can refer to both prawns and shrimps, but this recipe specifically calls for brown shrimp — small shellfish with a nicely pronounced flavour that when raw are greyish-brown but flush with vibrant shades of pink and orange after cooking. The salty marine tang of the samphire (sea beans) serves as a perfect foil for the tiny, slightly sweet shellfish. Prepared and cooked in a matter of minutes, with only a few ingredients and a minimum of fuss, this is a perfect quick lunch or supper dish.

Preparation time: 5 minutes
Cooking time: 10 minutes
Serves: 2

- juice of 1 lemon
- 125 g / 4½ oz (1⅛ sticks) butter, diced
- 100 g / 3½ oz samphire (sea beans), washed (tough stems removed if necessary)
- 100 g / 3½ oz cooked brown shrimps (crevette)
- black pepper

Bring a large saucepan of water to the boil, ready for blanching the samphire (sea beans).

Put the lemon juice into a small saucepan set over a low heat and whisk in the butter slowly, a little at a time, with a hand whisk. This will take 4–5 minutes. Avoid bringing it to the boil. Season with pepper and set aside.

Blanch the samphire in the boiling water for 1–2 minutes, drain and mix with the brown shrimps in a bowl. Divide the shrimps and samphire between two plates, drizzle the warm lemony butter sauce over them and serve immediately.

GF

Blue cheese, chicory, pear and walnut salad

This classic, light starter (appetizer) is very quick to prepare and is a perfect way to use the chicory bulbs whose season in the UK peaks during the autumn (fall) months. Half of the blue cheese is blended with olive oil, white wine vinegar and warm water to make a deliciously creamy dressing for the salad, whose salty punchiness is the perfect foil for the crisp, slightly bitter chicory leaves and the sweet pears. The walnuts add crunch and earthiness to the dish. This recipe is inspired and adapted from one by Raymond Blanc. You can substitute apples for the pears if you like.

Preparation time: 15 minutes
Serves: 4

- 2 pears, ripe but firm, halved, cored and sliced thinly
- 775 g / 1¾ lb small bulbs white and purple chicory (endive), washed, trimmed and leaves separated
- 80 g / 3 oz (⅔ cup) coarsely chopped walnuts, toasted
- 80 g / 3 oz cold blue cheese (such as Roquefort or Stilton), crumbled
- 1 tablespoon snipped chives

For the dressing:

- 80 g / 3 oz blue cheese (such as Roquefort or Stilton)
- 2 tablespoons warm water
- 1½ tablespoons red wine vinegar
- 2 tablespoons extra virgin olive oil
- a generous pinch of black pepper

First, make the dressing. Put the blue cheese into a large bowl and cream it to a smooth paste, using a wooden spoon. Add the warm water and vinegar and whisk until combined, then gradually whisk in the olive oil and season with the black pepper.

Add the pears, chicory (endive) and walnuts and toss to with your hands to coat in the dressing. Sprinkle the crumbled cheese and snipped chives on top of the salad and serve.

GF

Fennel and crab linguine

In the UK the crab season stretches from April until November, but September and October are the best months to get the largest and fattest crabs at the best prices. For convenience I usually buy the white and brown meat ready prepared, but from time to time there is something very satisfying about the meticulous process of picking the meat from a whole cooked crab. The white meat is sweeter than the meatier brown and the gentle aniseed flavour of the fennel complements the delicate nuttiness of the crab in this indulgent pasta dish, which is my own take on a River Café recipe.

Preparation time: 10 minutes
Cooking time: 15 minutes
Serves: 6

- 2 fennel bulbs (keep any leafy tops)
- 50 g / 2 oz (3½ tablespoons) butter
- 300 g / 11 oz white crabmeat
- 100 g / 3½ oz brown crabmeat
- 1 red chilli (chile), seeded and finely chopped
- juice of 1 small lemon
- 2 cloves garlic, finely chopped
- handful flat-leaf parsley, coarsely chopped
- 400 g / 14 oz fresh or dry linguine
- 30 ml / 1 fl oz (2 tablespoons) extra virgin olive oil
- sea salt and black pepper

Remove the outer layers of the fennel bulbs, then thinly slice the bulbs lengthwise. Remove the leaves from the fennel tops, chop the leaves coarsely and set aside.

Melt the butter in a frying pan (skillet) over a medium–low heat. Add the sliced fennel and sauté for 5 minutes until they are soft and lightly golden.

Mix the two crabmeats together in a bowl. Add the chilli (chile), lemon juice, garlic and parsley, season with salt and pepper and stir to mix. Cover with clingfilm (plastic wrap) and set aside in the refrigerator while you cook the pasta.

Bring a generous amount of salted water to the boil in a large saucepan. Add the pasta and cook until al dente (fresh pasta will take less time to cook than dry pasta), drain it and return it to the saucepan. Stir the crab mix into the pasta and add the sautéed fennel. Drizzle with the extra virgin olive oil and sprinkle over the chopped fennel leaves. Season with salt and pepper and serve straight away.

Wild mushroom risotto

This recipe uses both fresh and dried mushrooms. There are more than 14,000 species of wild mushroom growing in the UK (not all of which are edible) and the main mushroom season in the UK covers the period September to November, although there are varieties that can be foraged throughout the year. Dried mushrooms are a larder (pantry) staple for me. Rehydrating them produces a rich, earthy-coloured steeping liquid, which is a flavourful and versatile ingredient in itself. This recipe uses this dried mushroom broth with chicken stock (broth) as it's something I often have to hand, but it is equally tasty made with vegetable stock and is then suitable for vegetarians.

Preparation time: 10 minutes, plus 40 minutes rehydrating/soaking time
Cooking time: 35 minutes
Serves: 4–6

- 200 g / 7 oz dried porcini
- 750 g / 1½ lb mixed wild mushrooms, washed in cold water and trimmed
- 1 litre / 34 fl oz (4¼ cups) chicken stock (broth)
- 100 g / 3½ oz (7 tablespoons) butter
- 1 onion, finely chopped
- 2 cloves garlic, crushed
- 450 g / 1 lb (2⅓ cups) arborio or carnaroli rice
- 150 g / 5 oz Parmesan cheese, freshly grated
- sea salt and black pepper

To serve:
- handful snipped chives
- freshly grated Parmesan cheese

Put the dried porcini in a heatproof bowl and cover with boiling water to allow them to rehydrate for 40 minutes. Remove the porcini from the soaking liquid, keeping the liquid to one side and straining it to remove any grit. Coarsely slice all the mixed wild mushrooms and the porcini so they are more or less the same size.

Pour the stock (broth) and the mushroom steeping liquid into a saucepan, bring it gently to the boil and maintain at a simmer.

Put half the butter into another saucepan, add the onion and garlic and cook over a low heat for 5–10 minutes until the onion is soft and translucent, then add the rice. Stir to coat the rice well in the butter, then add both the dry and fresh mushrooms. Add the stock, ladle by ladle, stirring continuously as you do so, allowing each ladleful to be absorbed before adding the next. Continue for about 20 minutes until the rice is cooked but still firm to the bite.

Remove from the heat and season well with salt and pepper. Stir in the remaining butter and the Parmesan and sprinkle over the chives. Leave the risotto to rest for a minute before serving. Serve with an extra bowl of grated Parmesan.

Fillet of beef with anchovy brown butter and wild greens

In this recipe for roast beef from her *Spring* cookbook, Skye Gyngell replaces a traditional gravy accompaniment with a warm savoury dressing that could hardly be simpler to make. Canned anchovies are melted into foaming butter, red wine vinegar is added once the sauce has thickened slightly and seasonal greens are stirred in for just as long as it takes for them to wilt down. Rich in umami flavours, it is the preserved anchovies that give this dish its earthy, unmistakably autumnal character.

Preparation time: 10 minutes
Cooking time: 15 minutes
Serves: 4

- 800–850 g / 1¾–2 lb whole beef fillet (tenderloin), trimmed
- a splash of olive oil
- 100 g / 3½ oz (7 tablespoons) unsalted butter
- 2 × 50-g / 2-oz cans anchovies (Ortiz are my favourite)
- 2 tablespoons red wine vinegar
- 2 handfuls wild greens, or a mixture of rocket (arugula) and dandelion
- sea salt and black pepper

Preheat the oven to 200°C / 400°F / Gas Mark 6.

Season the meat really generously all over with salt and pepper. This is important as the sea salt combined with a high heat will give the beef a deliciously textural, crunchy outer coating.

Place a heavy frying pan (skillet), large enough to hold the whole piece of beef, over a high heat. When the pan begins to smoke, add the oil and swirl the pan to coat the base well. Add the meat and brown really well all over; this is best achieved by leaving the meat alone — if you push it around the pan it will stew rather than form a crust. Once the meat is really well browned, transfer it to a roasting pan and place on the middle shelf of the oven to finish cooking for 5 minutes.

Meanwhile, place the butter in a heavy nonstick frying pan over a high heat and allow it to melt and begin to foam. As soon as the butter begins to colour (and smell deliciously nutty), add the anchovies and stir vigorously until they disintegrate and become a part of the sauce.

When the meat is cooked, remove it from the oven and set aside in a warm place to rest while you wilt the greens.

Once the anchovies have melted into the sauce and thickened it slightly, add the wine vinegar. Now add the greens and cook briefly, stirring, to just wilt the vegetables. Set aside.

To serve, cut the meat into thick slices, allowing 3 slices per person. Arrange on warm plates and spoon the sauce and wilted greens over the top. Serve at once.

GF

Roasted butternut squash with wilted greens and pine nuts

I love dishes where you roast a mixture of vegetables in one pan — it saves on washing up, but also produces wonderful flavours and colours. Combinations I like to cook include fennel and spinach; cauliflower, fennel and butternut squash; courgette (zucchini) and tomatoes; carrots and parsnips; and mushrooms and Jerusalem artichokes (see page 188) with welcome added texture from toasted pine nuts. The trick is to always start by roasting the vegetables that take longer to cook and to add the quicker-cooking ones partway through.

Preparation time: 10 minutes
Cooking time: 25–30 minutes
Serves: 6 as a side dish

- 1 × 700-g / 1 lb 8½-oz butternut squash, peeled, seeded and diced
- 5 shallots, peeled and halved
- 3 tablespoons olive oil
- large bunch spinach, kale, cavolo nero (Tuscan kale) or beetroot (beet) leaves, washed and thick stems removed
- 2 tablespoons toasted pine nuts
- sea salt and black pepper

Preheat the oven to 180°C / 350°F / Gas Mark 4. Put the butternut squash and shallots into a roasting pan, drizzle with the oil and toss to coat. Season with salt and pepper and roast in the oven for 20–25 minutes until the squash and shallots are soft and beginning to turn brown, turning them once during this time. Remove from the oven and stir in the green vegetables. Return to the oven for another 5 minutes until the green vegetables have wilted, then remove from the oven, sprinkle with the pine nuts and serve.

Vegetable curry

As more of my family become vegan and vegetarian, I am always looking for recipes that will please everyone. The key to this recipe is to use the ripest, sweetest tomatoes, while the spices and vegetables can be adjusted to suit your taste. The flavours of the curry will deepen and improve if the dish is made in advance. I like to serve it with saffron rice and flatbreads.

Preparation time: 15 minutes, plus 30 minutes resting time
Cooking time: 50 minutes
Serves: 4

- 4 or 5 large ripe beef (beefsteak) tomatoes, peeled and coarsely chopped
- 4 white onions, peeled, halved and thinly sliced
- about 100 ml / 3½ fl oz (⅓ cup plus 1 tablespoon) olive oil
- 2 aubergines (eggplants), cut into smallish cubes
- 2 teaspoons fenugreek seeds
- 2 teaspoons fennel seeds
- 2 teaspoons black mustard seeds
- 2 teaspoons coriander seeds
- 2 teaspoons cumin seeds
- 6 cardamom pods
- 6 cloves
- 5 cloves garlic, finely chopped
- 3-cm (1¼-inch) piece of fresh ginger, peeled and finely grated
- 2 fresh red chillies (chiles), finely chopped
- 1 tablespoon ground coriander
- 1 tablespoon ground turmeric
- a little vegetable stock (broth) (optional)
- 350 g / 12 oz fine French beans
- sea salt and black pepper

To serve:
- Flatbreads (page 099)
- cooked rice

Sprinkle the chopped tomatoes with salt and pepper and leave for at least 30 minutes before you use them (the longer the better).

Preheat the oven to 180°C / 350°F / Gas Mark 4.

Put the sliced onion in a large, heavy casserole dish with about 4 tablespoons of the olive oil. Fry over a low heat for 30 minutes, stirring regularly until they begin to turn brown.

While the onions are cooking, put the cubed aubergine (eggplant) into a roasting pan, toss with the rest of the olive oil and roast in the oven for about 25 minutes until they are soft and cooked.

Put all the whole dry spices (not the ground coriander or turmeric) into a dry frying pan (skillet) over a low heat and fry until they begin to crackle and burst (being careful not to burn them). Remove from the heat and, when they have cooled, put them into a spice grinder or use a pestle and mortar and grind to a powder.

When the onions are ready, stir in the freshly toasted and ground spices and cook for a few more minutes. Add the garlic, ginger, chillies (chiles), ground coriander and turmeric. After 20 seconds, add the tomatoes. Simmer for about 20 minutes until the tomatoes are soft and some of the juices have evaporated and the colour begins to darken. Add the roasted aubergines, mix everything together and heat gently. You can add some vegetable stock (broth), if you want more liquid.

Just before you are ready to eat, steam the French beans for about 4 minutes until tender, then stir them into the casserole dish. Season to taste with salt and pepper and serve with flatbread and cooked rice on the side.

VG

Fish pie

Fish pie is the ultimate comfort food — buttery mashed potatoes piled on top of a base of flaked smoked fish in a creamy, wine sauce, with scallops and prawns (shrimp) thrown in to make it extra special. Combining smoked with unsmoked fish brings a wonderful depth of flavour to this dish.

Preparation time: 15 minutes
Cooking time: 1 hour
Serves: 6

- 400 ml / 14 fl oz (1⅔ cups) milk
- pinch of sea salt
- 2 bay leaves
- 1 teaspoon black peppercorns
- 500 g / 1 lb 2 oz smoked haddock fillet, skin on
- 500 g / 1 lb 2 oz salmon fillet, skin on
- 100 g / 3½ oz uncooked scallops, trimmed of their orange 'skirts' and any white gristle removed
- 100 g / 3½ oz uncooked shelled prawns (shrimp)
- sea salt and black pepper

For the béchamel sauce:
- 60 g / 2 oz (4¼ tablespoons) unsalted butter, plus some extra tiny pieces for baking
- 50 g / 2½ oz (⅓ cup plus 1 tablespoon) plain (all-purpose) flour
- 1 heaped teaspoon Dijon mustard
- 30 ml / 1 fl oz (1¾ tablespoons) white wine

For the mashed potatoes:
- 1.5 kg / 3¼ lb maincrop (main-season) potatoes, peeled (halved or quartered if large)
- 50 g / 2 oz (3½ tablespoons) unsalted butter
- 100 g / 3½ oz (½ cup) crème fraîche
- 100 ml / 3½ fl oz (⅓ cup plus 1 tablespoon) milk

To serve:
- handful snipped chives
- cooked peas
- cooked samphire (sea beans)

Pour the milk into a large sauté pan and add the salt, bay leaves, and peppercorns. Add the haddock, skin side down. Poach the haddock in the milk over a low heat for 4 minutes, turning it onto the flesh side for another 2 minutes once the skin side is cooked. Remove the haddock from the milk with a slotted spoon and set aside. Poach the salmon in the same way, using the same milk. Remove the salmon from the pan and allow to cool before removing the skin from both the salmon and haddock. Strain the poaching liquid into a bowl and set aside. When the fish is cool enough, flake it coarsely into a bowl.

Slice each scallop into 2 or 3 round discs and place them into a 2.5-litre / 84-fl oz (10½-cup) gratin dish. Add the shelled uncooked prawns (shrimp) and the flaked fish and set aside.

To make the béchamel sauce, melt the butter in a medium nonstick saucepan over a medium–low heat, add the flour, stir and allow the roux to cook for a minute, then add the mustard. Gradually stir in the wine, followed by the fish poaching liquid, stirring constantly to avoid lumps forming, and simmer over a low heat for about 10 minutes until thickened. Taste to check the seasoning and remove from the heat.

To prepare the mashed potatoes, bring a large saucepan of salted water to the boil. Add the potatoes and cook until tender, then drain in a colander and leave the surface moisture to evaporate for a minute. Mash the potatoes with a potato masher or pass them through a sieve. Add the butter, crème fraîche and milk and continue to mash it all together until it is smooth.

When the béchamel sauce is cool, spoon it over the fish and then spoon the mashed potatoes over the top. Smooth the surface, then use a fork to make furrows in the mash. You can cover and chill the pie at this point for up to 24 hours until required.

To cook, preheat the oven to 190°C / 375°F / Gas Mark 5, add tiny pieces of butter to the top of the pie and bake for 40–45 minutes until it is crusty and golden on the surface. Remove from the oven and serve sprinkled with some snipped chives and cooked peas with samphire (sea beans) on the side.

Jerusalem artichokes with mushrooms and spinach

This wholesome and earthy vegetable dish works well as a side dish, but it is sufficiently substantial to serve as a main meal, too. The sweetness of the artichokes is balanced by the rich savouriness of the mushrooms and spinach.

Preparation time: 10 minutes
Cooking time: 45 minutes
Serves: 6 as a side dish

- 500 g / 1 lb 2 oz Jerusalem artichokes, scrubbed (unpeeled)
- 4 shallots, quartered
- 4 cloves garlic, coarsely chopped
- 8 tablespoons olive oil
- 10 sprigs thyme
- juice of 1 lemon
- 300 g / 11 oz portobello or button mushrooms, thickly sliced
- 300 g / 11 oz (10 cups) spinach
- sea salt and black pepper

Preheat the oven to 180°C / 350°F / Gas Mark 4.

Cut the Jerusalem artichokes into pieces of more or less the same size and put them into a roasting pan with the shallots and garlic. Drizzle over the half of the olive oil, add the thyme sprigs and lemon juice and use your hands to coat the vegetables thoroughly. Season generously with salt and pepper and roast in the oven for 25–30 minutes until the artichokes and shallots are soft and beginning to turn brown.

Remove from the oven and add the sliced mushrooms. Drizzle with the remaining olive oil and stir everything together. Roast for another 15 minutes until the mushrooms have shrunk in size and softened. Remove from the oven and stir in the spinach. Return the pan to the oven for about 3 minutes to allow the spinach to wilt, then season to taste, remove the thyme sprigs and serve.

GF

Caramelized fennel

Fennel is rich in dietary fibre, minerals, vitamins and phytonutrients. A member of the carrot family, it also has the advantage of being cholesterol-free. This recipe is from Maya Even. Sweet and succulent, here the fennel is roasted slowly at a low temperature until it becomes meltingly caramelized. Fennel's gentle aniseed flavour makes it the perfect accompaniment to roast chicken or grilled fish. Although I include the recipe as a side dish here, it can easily steal the show and certainly has the stature to form the heart of a vegetarian lunch or supper.

Preparation time: 10 minutes
Cooking time: 50 minutes
Serves: 6 as a side dish

- 3 fennel bulbs, stalks and fronds removed and reserved to garnish
- 80 g / 3 oz (5½ tablespoons) butter
- 4 tablespoons olive oil
- 1 tablespoon caster (superfine) sugar
- 2 tablespoons Pernod or vermouth
- sea salt and black pepper

Preheat the oven to 150°C / 300°F / Gas Mark 2.

Holding the fennel bulbs upright, cut them neatly into 1-cm (½-inch)-thick slices, then place in a single layer in a large ovenproof sauté pan that has a lid.

Put the butter and oil into a small saucepan over a medium heat and once the butter has melted, pour it over the fennel. Sprinkle the sugar on top.

Sauté the fennel over a medium heat for about 5 minutes on each side, turning the slices carefully to maintain their shape. Turn off the heat and pour over the Pernod or vermouth. Put a lid on the pan and roast in the oven for about 40 minutes until the fennel is tender and caramelized. Alternatively, the final stage of cooking can be completed on the hob (stove). Season with salt and pepper, garnish with the fennel fronds and trimmed stalks and serve.

GF

Braised red cabbage

This recipe cooks itself. It is simply a matter of assembling the ingredients in a large casserole dish with a lid and leaving it in the oven until it's done. The secret to its success for me is balancing sweet with sour and braising the cabbage long enough for it to be tender but not reduced to a mush. Other combinations of spices also work well, such as star anise. This dish is an excellent accompaniment to hot or cold roasted meats, but it has a particular affinity with ham. While it can be eaten as soon as it is cooked, it will only have improved if consumed a day or two later.

Preparation time: 10 minutes
Cooking time: 1 hour 30 minutes
Serves: 6 as a side dish

- 3 small red onions, finely sliced
- 3 crisp eating (dessert) apples, cored and finely sliced
- ½ red cabbage, outer leaves and core removed, finely shredded
- 1 cinnamon stick
- 6 cloves
- 2 tablespoons red wine vinegar
- 1 tablespoon soft brown sugar
- 250 ml / 8 fl oz (1 cup) apple juice
- 15 g / ½ oz (1 tablespoon) butter
- sea salt and black pepper

Put the onions and apples into the bottom of a large casserole dish. Add the cabbage, spices, vinegar and sugar and pour the apple juice over the top. Dot the butter on top and put the lid on the casserole dish, transfer to the oven and bake for 1 hour 30 minutes, stirring the mix once or twice until it is cooked.

Remove from the oven, season with salt and pepper, remove the cloves and cinnamon stick and serve.

Caprese cake

Torta caprese is a flourless chocolate cake made with almonds or walnuts that originates from the Mediterranean island of Capri. The use of ground almonds (almond meal) in place of flour produces a cake which is crispy on the outside and soft and slightly chewy on the inside, with the added advantage of also being gluten free. Because the cake is so moist, it can be eaten on its own, but I prefer to serve it with poached quince or fresh berries and a dollop of crème fraîche.

Preparation time: 20 minutes
Cooking time: 45 minutes
Serves: 8

- 4 eggs
- 160 g / 5½ oz (¾ cup) caster (superfine) sugar
- 1 teaspoon vanilla extract
- 250 g / 9 oz (2½ cups) ground almonds (almond meal)
- 50 g / 2 oz (½ cup) coarsely chopped almonds
- 180 g / 6½ oz dark (semisweet) chocolate, finely chopped or grated
- 200 g / 7¼ oz (1¾ sticks) unsalted butter, melted and cooled, plus extra for greasing

To serve:
- 1½ tablespoons icing (confectioners') sugar
- Poached quince (page 203) or fresh seasonal berries
- crème fraîche

Preheat the oven to 180°C / 350°F / Gas Mark 4. Grease a 24-cm (9¾-inch) round cake pan with butter and line with greaseproof (wax) paper.

Put the eggs into a bowl with the sugar and vanilla extract and beat for about 10 minutes until pale yellow and fluffy. Gently fold in the ground almonds (almond meal), chopped almonds, chocolate and butter, folding after each addition until they are all combined.

Spoon the mixture into the prepared cake pan, level out the top with an offset palette knife (spatula) or the back of the spoon and bake in the oven for 45 minutes until the cake is firm to the touch. Remove from the oven and leave to cool in the pan, then turn out onto a cooling rack.

Sift the icing (confectioners') sugar directly over the cake and serve with slices of poached quince or fresh berries and crème fraîche.

VG

Fig tart

This recipe is taken from Skye Gyngell's cookbook *How I Cook*. It is a classic French tart filled a with pastry cream. As Skye says, you can vary the fruit according to the season, using lightly poached apricots or peaches, halved strawberries or whole raspberries.

—

Preparation time: 30 minutes, plus 1 hour cooling and chilling time
Cooking time: 35 minutes
Serves: 6

For the pastry:
- 250 g / 9 oz (2 cups) plain unbleached (all-purpose) flour, sifted, plus extra to dust
- 125 g / 4½ oz (1⅛ sticks) unsalted butter, well chilled, cut into small cubes
- 1 tablespoon caster (superfine) sugar
- 1 teaspoon vanilla extract
- 1 organic, free-range egg yolk
- a little iced water

For the pastry cream:
- 320 ml / 10¾ fl oz (1⅓ cups) milk
- 3 organic, free-range egg yolks
- 2–3 drops vanilla extract
- 3 tablespoons caster (superfine) sugar
- 3 tablespoons plain (all-purpose) flour
- 15 g / ½ oz (1 tablespoon) chilled unsalted butter, cut into pieces

For the topping:
- 8 perfectly ripe figs, washed
- 1 tablespoon fig, strawberry or raspberry jam (preserves)

VG

To make the pastry dough, tip the flour into a food processor and add the chilled butter, sugar and vanilla extract. Pulse until you have the consistency of coarse breadcrumbs. Add the egg yolk and 1 tablespoon of iced water and pulse once more; the pastry dough should begin to come together. Add a little more iced water as necessary, pulsing until the pastry dough forms a ball.

Wrap the pastry dough in baking (parchment) paper or clingfilm (plastic wrap) and leave to rest in the refrigerator for 30 minutes.

To make the pastry cream, gently warm the milk in a saucepan over a low heat until it just emits a little steam. Meanwhile, whisk the egg yolks, vanilla extract, sugar and flour together in a bowl to combine. Slowly pour on the warm milk, whisking as you do so.

Pour the mixture back into the pan and stir continuously over a low heat, using a wooden spoon in a figure-of-eight motion, until the custard thickens enough to coat the back of the spoon and no longer tastes floury; this will take about 10 minutes. Immediately pour through a sieve into a clean heatproof bowl and whisk in the chilled butter. Leave to cool completely, then cover the surface with baking parchment or clingfilm and refrigerate.

Roll out the pastry dough on a floured surface to a round 3 mm (⅛ inch) thick. Carefully lift the dough onto the rolling pin and drape it over a 25 cm (10 inch) fluted tart pan, about 3 cm (1¼ inches) deep. Press the pastry gently into the fluted sides and prick the base with a fork. Return to the refrigerator to chill for another 30 minutes.

Preheat the oven to 180°C / 350°F / Gas Mark 4. Line the pastry case with greaseproof (wax) paper and baking beans (pie weights) and bake 'blind' in the oven for 20 minutes. Remove the paper and beans and return to the oven for 15 minutes, or until the pastry is cooked through, golden and crisp. Transfer to a cooling rack and leave to cool completely.

Spoon the pastry cream into the cooled pastry case and spread it evenly. Slice the figs across into rounds and lay them, overlapping, on top of the pastry cream in a circular pattern. Warm the jam (preserves) with 2 tablespoons of water in a small saucepan, stirring to dissolve, then bring to the boil. Remove from the heat and allow to cool slightly. Using a pastry brush, gently brush the figs with the glaze. Cut into generous slices to serve.

Madeleines

Originating from the Lorraine region of northeastern France, madeleines were famously cherished by the writer Proust, as a catalyst for the release of childhood memories. These traditional shell-shaped sponge cakes are delicious served with a cup of tea or as an accompaniment to a dessert.

Preparation time: 30 minutes, plus 6 hours (or overnight) chilling time
Cooking time: 7–9 minutes
Makes: 12 madeleines

- grated zest of 2 lemons
- 60 g / 2 oz (¼ cup plus 1 tablespoon) caster (superfine) sugar
- 75 g / 2¾ oz (½ cup plus 1½ tablespoons) plain (all-purpose) flour, plus extra for dusting
- pinch of salt
- 2 teaspoons baking powder
- 2 eggs
- 35 g / 1¼ oz (5 teaspoons) acacia or other runny honey
- 100 g / 3½ oz (7 tablespoons) unsalted butter, melted and cooled, plus an extra tablespoon for brushing
- icing (confectioners') sugar, for dusting

Mix the lemon zest with the sugar and set aside.

Sift the flour, salt and baking powder together into a bowl. Put the eggs, honey, lemon zest and sugar into the bowl of a stand mixer fitted with the whisk attachment and whisk until the mixture has increased in volume and is light and frothy. Remove the bowl from the stand mixer and fold in the flour mix, then lightly whisk in the melted butter. Cover the bowl with clingfilm (plastic wrap) and refrigerate the batter for at least 6 hours or overnight.

When ready to bake, melt the extra tablespoon of butter and brush the hollows of a 12-hole madeleine pan with a pastry brush. Place the pan in the refrigerator for 15 minutes to allow the butter to harden, then sprinkle with flour.

Preheat the oven to 200°C / 400°F / Gas Mark 6.

Spoon the chilled batter into the moulds in the prepared pan until each is three-quarters full. Place in the top third of the oven to bake for 7–9 minutes until the madeleines are risen and golden. Remove from the oven and leave for 1–2 minutes before lifting them out of the pan.

Serve the madeleines warm, with a light dusting of icing (confectioners') sugar.

VG

Autumn crumble

When I make this dish I combine whatever fruits are in season and available, which usually includes windfall apples and pears from the Home Farm orchard and foraged blackberries. For a few precious weeks, the hedgerows in the surrounding Oxfordshire countryside are studded with berries that, while not as large as the commercially grown alternatives, are full of flavour. A small party of pickers with baskets and tubs can quickly amass a sufficient harvest for both baking and preserving. Any berries that are not destined for immediate use can be bagged up and stored in the freezer for the months ahead.

Preparation time: 15 minutes
Cooking time: 20–25 minutes
Serves: 4–6

- 300 g / 11 oz (2 cups) blackberries
- 2 Granny Smith apples, peeled, cored and sliced
- 2 firm Comice or Conference pears, peeled, cored and sliced
- 2 tablespoons caster (superfine) sugar
- squeeze of lemon juice
- 100 g / 3½ oz (7 tablespoons) cold unsalted butter, diced
- double (heavy) cream or vanilla ice cream, to serve

For the crumble (crumb) topping:
- 100 g / 3½ oz (½ cup) light brown sugar
- 1 teaspoon baking powder
- 3 tablespoons quick-cook porridge (rolled) oats
- 125 g / 4½ oz (1 cup) plain (all-purpose) flour

Preheat the oven to 180°C / 350°F / Gas Mark 4.

Put the fruits, caster (superfine) sugar, lemon juice and a few cubes of the butter into a 27-cm / 11-inch baking dish and combine with your hands.

To make the crumble (crumb) topping, put the sugar, baking powder, oats and flour into a bowl and mix well. Add the remaining butter and rub it into the dry mixture with your fingertips until the mixture resembles coarse breadcrumbs. Spread the crumble evenly over the fruit and bake in the oven for 20–25 minutes until golden brown and bubbling.

Remove from the oven and serve warm, with double (heavy) cream or vanilla ice cream.

VG

Poached quince

Quince are the golden apples of mythology and the fruit with which, according to Jewish tradition, Eve tempted Adam. In southern Europe and the Middle East, the pear- or apple-shaped fruit can be picked soft, perfumed and golden straight from the branch, but in our cooler northern climes, quince are ripened off the tree and its lumpy yellow skin and hard, bitter flesh should not be eaten raw. The addition of generous quantities of sugar and the application of gentle heat, however, bring out its aromatic delicacy.

Preparation time: 10 minutes
Cooking time: 1 hour 10 minutes
Serves: 6

- 200 g / 7 oz (¾ cup plus 1 tablespoon) demerara sugar
- rind and juice of 3 unwaxed lemons
- 2 cinnamon sticks
- 3 star anise
- 3 quince, washed, peeled, halved and cored (keep the skins and cores)
- ice cream, to serve

Combine 1 litre / 34 fl oz (4¼ cups) water and the sugar in a saucepan. Add the lemon rind, lemon juice and spices to the pan, then add the peeled, halved quince with the peeled skins and cores. Cover the quince with a sheet of greaseproof (wax) paper and cover the pan with a lid. Simmer over a low heat for 30 minutes, then turn the quince over and simmer for another 30 minutes, or until the fruit is soft but still holds its shape. Remove the fruit from the pan using a slotted spoon and set aside.

Return the pan to the heat and boil the liquid for about 10 minutes to reduce it to a syrup. Allow to cool, then remove the aromatics from the pan, before returning the quince to the liquid. Serve the quince and the syrup with ice cream.

GF

Winter

'If light is scarce then light is scarce; we will immerse ourselves in the darkness and there discover its own particular beauty.'

Jun'ichirō Tanizaki, *In Praise of Shadows*

—

I spend autumn (fall) dreading the arrival of winter. I think this is because I was brought up in the southern hemisphere. As a child, Christmas was always spent outdoors and barefoot. When winter does finally sweep in, however, with its short days and spirit-testing weather, it has its own magic and stark beauty. The views around Home Farm are pared to the simplicity of vast skies and the underlying contours of the ground. With the disappearance of the rusty burnished tones of autumn, the bare forms of the trees dominate the landscape, bleached by mist or starkly silhouetted, some strung with spheres of mistletoe. Meantime, in the woods, the holly is bright with berries. Winter is a season of contrasts. It is a season of dank, muddy walks and time spent quietly in front of a blazing fire with just a book for company, but just as the urge to hibernate becomes irresistible, so Christmas arrives, with its convivial gatherings of family and friends.

The winter solstice — the shortest day of the year, when the sun and moon appear to stand still in the sky — falls a few days before Christmas. It is a time to appreciate the significance of stillness, darkness and cold.

As we adapt to the dwindling days and changing larder (pantry), so we make adjustments to the way we prepare and cook food. While we spend more time indoors, it feels natural for our rituals to become slower and more considered. We mirror in these more protracted rhythms the underlying slowness of the season: there is little point in trying to outpace or counter nature. The ingredients we associate with winter tend to be deep and robustly flavoured, well-suited to extended cooking processes — to roasting, braising, baking and stewing. There is something wonderfully nostalgic about the smell of smoke from the wood burner drifting from room to room, combining with the aromas of a chicken pie, a gently simmering casserole or soup and the scent of a chocolate cake, freshly out of the oven and cooling on the side. At the same time, the occasional craving for the fresh, barely cooked dishes of the warmer months, bright with chilli (chile) and lime — heartening, energy-enhancing reminders of long summer days — can be satisfied within a broader commitment to the mood and produce of the season.

Home Farm comes into its own at Christmas, as family and friends gather around the table and fires burn in hearths and stoves throughout the house to counter the deep cold outside (overleaf).

The local farm shops are filled with an amazing variety of root vegetables and cabbages: Brussels sprouts, Jerusalem artichokes, cavolo nero (Tuscan kale), parsnips, Belgian endive, leeks, potatoes, red cabbage, celeriac (celery root), kale, shallots, swede (rutabaga), Savoy cabbage, squash, turnips and celery. In January and February come spring greens, and purple sprouting broccoli (broccolini) and chervil are at their best. The sweet chestnut season that starts in October peaks in December. For those who eat meat, a wide range of game is available — venison, partridge, pigeon, guinea fowl, pheasant and grouse. Meantime, it is easy to forget that cheese, in its artisan forms, is an entirely seasonal product, with the rhythms of grazing cows, sheep and goats intimately connected with the cycle of the year. In specialist cheese shops, you can now find tangy Mont d'Or in its wooden box, pungent Stilton — made in the summer and reaching its peak in December, when it is delicious served with walnuts and celery — extra-mature Cheddars, like Montgomery, Westcombe and Keens, Chevrotin des Aravis made with goat's milk, Comté, Époisses de Bourgogne and the sweet nuttiness of Gruyère.

Amidst the unfolding narrative of festive rituals — the decorating of the tree, the preparing of food, the wrapping of presents — Home Farm retains its underlying sense of calm and ease.

The festive period is about abundance and indulgence, when even those committed to sourcing local ingredients are tempted to look further afield. It is always a joyful moment when Moroccan blood oranges start to arrive, just before Christmas, joining the mandarins, Seville oranges and clementines as reminders of warmer times. The jars of cinnamon, cloves, nutmeg and star anise are regularly brought out from the shelves of the Home Farm larder (pantry), along with preserved fruits, to be added to Christmas puddings, mince pies, brandy butter and fruit cakes.

I still feel child-like excitement at the approach of Christmas. I get completely swept up in the preparations of choosing and wrapping presents, decorating the house and collecting and stringing a big Christmas tree with fairy lights. This is the one time of the year when John indulges my desire for over-decoration. I pick armfuls of mistletoe to hang from beams and cut holly, greenery and black hellebores — also known as Christmas roses — for the festive table. We are a large family. Our grandson was born recently and there are now four generations of the family, spanning ten decades. With friends, there are sometimes twenty people sitting around the Christmas table. The preparation of the food is planned with military precision and everyone helps. In our family the preference is for either goose or roast beef, instead of the traditional turkey, alongside which is a hearty nut loaf, prepared for vegetarians but enjoyed by everyone. The meal stretches long into the afternoon, with games played afterwards and presents unwrapped.

Four generations of family, spanning nearly a century, sit down together to share the celebratory goose or rib of beef.

After the joyful commotion of Christmas, there is a pause before the revelry of New Year. It is a time for me to write down my New Year's resolutions, which seem to be more or less the same every year. Our children disappear to more excitement than we can offer and we often spend New Year's Eve with just a couple of friends, reflecting on the past year and what the New Year will bring.

Following the indulgence of the festive period, January is a time for bringing back balance and restraint and turning to more simple food, for soothing soups, sustaining vegetables and nourishing lentils and pulses. As soon as we have passed the winter solstice, things can only get better for this girl from the southern hemisphere, with a minute or two of increasing daylight every day. Towards the end of January, snowdrops arrive with their nodding white flowers. We lift clumps out of the soil and bring them indoors in baskets, each a promise of the warmer times ahead.

Thyme and Gruyère gougères

These tasty, cheesy choux puffs are a perfect canapé. They can be made with any hard cheese you have to hand, such as Parmesan, Cheddar or Comté. My preference, however, is to use Gruyère, for its combination of sweet, salty and earthy notes. This recipe is inspired by food writer Felicity Cloake's gougères.

Preparation time: 30 minutes
Cooking time: 30 minutes
Makes: about 25 gougères

- 70 g / 2¾ oz (5 tablespoons) butter, cubed
- ¾ teaspoon fine salt
- 5 eggs
- 140 g / 4¾ oz (1 cup plus 2½ tablespoons) plain (all-purpose) flour, sifted
- 1 teaspoon English mustard powder
- 1 teaspoon thyme leaves
- 160 g / 5½ oz Gruyère or other hard cheese, finely grated
- 1 tablespoon milk

Line two baking sheets with baking (parchment) paper.

Pour 250 ml / 8 fl oz (1 cup) water into a saucepan, add the butter and salt and place over a medium heat. Simmer until the butter has melted. Meanwhile, whisk four of the eggs in a small bowl. Remove the pan from the heat and add the flour, beating it in with a wooden spoon until the mixture thickens. Return to the heat and stir for 2–3 minutes until the mixture forms a dough. Remove from the heat and use a wooden spoon to beat the dough for another 3–5 minutes until cool. Gradually beat in the whisked eggs, a little at a time, then stir in the mustard powder, thyme and Gruyère, reserving a little cheese for sprinkling later.

Preheat the oven to 180°C / 350°F / Gas Mark 4. Spoon the mixture into a piping (pastry) bag, snip off the end and pipe small dollops of the mixture onto the lined baking sheets, allowing enough space between each one for expansion (you should have enough mixture to make about 25 gougères). Whisk together the milk and fifth egg and brush onto the buns, then sprinkle with the reserved Gruyère and bake for 20 minutes. Briefly take them out and pierce each one with a fork or skewer and bake for another 5 minutes. Serve straight from the oven while still warm.

Anchovy toasts

Delicious salty anchovy crostini are the perfect snack to keep the wolf from the door while waiting for the main event. The anchovy butter will last for several weeks in the refrigerator and can be used for all sorts of dishes — slathered over broccoli or spinach, or a dollop of this tangy butter can also be served on top of lamb or beef. This recipe is inspired by one by the brilliant chef Yotam Ottolenghi. I like to use Ortiz anchovies, fished from the cold Atlantic waters off the north coast of Spain, which are salted, pressed and left to mature in barrels for six months, before being filleted and packed by hand.

Preparation time: 15 minutes
Makes: 10–12 toasts

- 8 canned anchovy fillets (preferably Ortiz), drained and coarsely chopped
- 1 clove garlic, finely chopped
- ½ green chilli (chile), seeded and finely chopped
- grated zest of 1 lemon and 1½ teaspoons lemon juice
- 80 g / 3 oz (5½ tablespoons) unsalted butter, softened
- 4 slices sourdough bread, grilled (broiled)
- olive oil, for drizzling
- handful flat-leaf parsley, finely chopped
- black pepper

Put the anchovies, garlic and chilli (chile) into the small bowl of a food processor, add the lemon juice and zest and process until smooth. Melt the butter in a small saucepan and, with the motor running, slowly pour it into the food processor to form an emulsified paste. Transfer it to a bowl and set aside.

Cut the slices of toast into 2-cm (¾-inch)-wide pieces to make it easy to eat with your fingers. Divide the butter mix among the toast pieces, spreading it generously. Drizzle with a little olive oil, garnish with the parsley, grind over some black pepper and serve at room temperature.

Roast rib of beef with Yorkshire puddings

For Christmas lunch, my family prefers to celebrate with the heartier, richer and more intense flavours of roast rib of beef rather than the traditional turkey. John is a Yorkshire man and his mother's Yorkshire puddings have passed into legend in his family. For eight people, I usually buy a 3-bone piece of rib, weighing 2.25–2.75 kg (5–6 lb) in total.

Preparation time: 30 minutes
Cooking time: about 1 hour 50 minutes, depending on weight of meat and how rare you want it
Serves: 8

- 1 × 3-bone rib of beef (standing rib roast)
- ½ teaspoon plain (all-purpose) flour
- ½ teaspoon English mustard powder
- 1 teaspoon rosemary leaves, finely chopped
- 4 cloves garlic, crushed
- sea salt and black pepper

For the horseradish sauce:
- 100 g / 3½ oz (¾ cup) crème fraîche
- 100 ml / 3½ fl oz (⅓ cup plus 1 tablespoon) double (heavy) cream, lightly whipped
- 2–3 teaspoons finely grated fresh horseradish
- sea salt

For the Yorkshire puddings:
- 110 g / 3¾ oz (¾ cup plus 1 tablespoon) plain (all-purpose) flour
- ½ teaspoon fine sea salt
- 2 eggs
- 150 ml / 5 fl oz (⅔ cup) milk
- 150 ml / 5 fl oz (⅔ cup) cold water
- dripping from the cooked beef

For the gravy:
- 1 tablespoon plain (all-purpose) flour
- 75 ml / 2½ fl oz (⅓ cup) red wine
- ½ teaspoon Dijon mustard
- 175 ml / 6 fl oz (¾ cup) beef stock (broth)

Take the beef out of the refrigerator at least an hour prior to cooking. Preheat the oven to 220°C / 425°F / Gas Mark 7.

Meanwhile, make the horseradish sauce by stirring the crème fraîche, whipped cream and horseradish together in a bowl and season to taste with salt. Cover and chill until ready to serve.

Place the rib, fat side down, in a hot frying pan (skillet) and sear the meat on all sides for a couple of minutes to seal in the juices. Sift the flour and mustard together and dust them over the beef. Place the beef in a roasting pan and season it with well with salt, pepper, some chopped rosemary leaves and the crushed garlic.

Roast the beef in the oven for 20 minutes, then reduce the heat to 190°C / 375°F / Gas Mark 5. Allow another 14 minutes per 500 g / 1 lb 2 oz for rare meat, basting it every 20–30 minutes with its juices.

When the meat has 30 minutes still to go, prepare the Yorkshire puddings. Sift the flour into a bowl from a height to allow it to air. Add the salt and form a well in the middle. Add the eggs and beat by hand with a whisk, gradually incorporating the flour. Combine the milk and water, then gradually add them, beating all the time, until you have a smooth and creamy batter. Leave the batter to rest for 30 minutes.

Remove the roasting pan from the oven and increase the oven temperature to the 220°C / 425°F / Gas Mark 7. Transfer the meat to a carving board, cover with aluminium foil and allow it to rest.

Meanwhile, skim any excess fat from the roasting juices in the pan and put a teaspoon into each compartment of a 12-hole muffin pan. Put the pan in the oven until it is sizzling hot, then fill each hole in the pan three-quarters full with the Yorkshire pudding batter and return to the oven. Cook for 15–20 minutes until golden and risen.

While the puddings are in the oven, prepare the gravy. Sprinkle the flour over the roasting juices and scrape up all the sticky bits from the bottom of the pan. Add the wine, stir in the mustard and then thin the gravy with the beef stock (broth). Simmer for several minutes on the stove then check the seasoning. Serve alongside the beef and Yorkshire puddings.

Chocolate, prune and whiskey cake

This is a recipe from Claire Ptak, who has the marvellous Violet bakery and café in east London. She is my favourite chef for baking as the recipes in her *The Violet Bakery Cookbook* are so easy to follow. The cake has no flour, so is gluten free and makes a very rich, gooey and boozy pudding for a special occasion. I choose this cake as an alternative to the traditional Christmas pudding and like to serve it with some cream.

Preparation time: 30 minutes, plus overnight soaking
Cooking time: 30–35 minutes,
Serves: 8

- 125 g / 4½ oz (¾ cup) stoned (pitted) Agen prunes
- 40 ml / 1⅓ fl oz (2¾ tablespoons) whiskey
- 240 g / 8½ oz dark (semisweet) chocolate (70% cocoa solids), chopped into small pieces
- 200 g / 7 oz (1¾ sticks) unsalted butter, plus extra for greasing
- 5 eggs, separated
- 100 g / 3½ oz (½ cup) caster (superfine) sugar
- 150 g / 5 oz (1½ cups) ground almonds (almond meal)
- ¼ teaspoon sea salt

VG GF

Soak the prunes in the whiskey. If you can do this the night before, so much the better.

Preheat the oven to 180°C / 350°F / Gas Mark 4. Butter a 20–23 cm (8–9 inch) cake pan and line it with baking (parchment) paper.

Put the chocolate and butter into a heatproof bowl and place over a pan of barely simmering water, making sure that the water does not touch the bottom of the bowl or it may spoil the chocolate. Stir occasionally to emulsify the butter and chocolate. Once the chocolate has melted, take the pan off the heat and allow to cool slightly, but keep away from any draughts.

Put the egg whites and yolks into two separate bowls. Starting with the yolks, add half the caster (superfine) sugar and whisk to thicken. Fold the thickened yolks into the melted chocolate, and set aside. Chop the prunes into eighths and add to the chocolate mixture along with the ground almonds (almond meal).

Beat the egg whites with the remaining caster sugar and sea salt until soft peaks form. Fold into the chocolate mixture until just incorporated. Pour into the prepared cake pan and bake for 30–35 minutes. The cake will be slightly soft in the middle but do not overbake it or the gooeyness will be lost.

Serve warm or at room temperature.

1

3

1 Thyme and Gruyère gougères
Anchovy toasts (below)

2 Roast rib of beef with Yorkshire puddings and horseradish sauce

3 Chocolate, prune and whiskey cake with cream

2

Courgette soup

The delicate green colour and heady hit of fresh herbs of this courgette (zucchini) soup, inspired by a classic River Café recipe, make it a welcome foil to winter's generally earthier palette and mellower flavours. I roast the courgettes in the oven as I like how it deepens their flavour, although this does add to the amount of washing up.

Preparation time: 10 minutes
Cooking time: 20–25 minutes
Serves: 6

- 1 kg / 2¼ lb courgettes (zucchini), trimmed and cut into pieces
- 60 ml / 2 fl oz (4 tablespoons) olive oil, plus extra to serve
- 2 cloves garlic, finely chopped
- 475 ml / 16 fl oz (2 cups) vegetable stock (broth)
- 100 g / 3½ oz Parmesan cheese, finely grated, plus extra to serve
- handful basil leaves, torn
- handful mint leaves, chopped
- 120 ml / 4 fl oz (½ cup) crème fraîche
- sea salt and black pepper
- toasted bread, to serve

Preheat the oven to 180°C / 350°F / Gas Mark 4. Put the courgettes (zucchini) into a roasting pan, drizzle with half the olive oil and toss with your hands to coat them in the oil. Add the garlic and season with salt. Roast in the oven for 15–20 minutes until soft and just beginning to turn brown, then tip the courgettes into a heavy saucepan with the remaining oil and place over a medium–low heat, then pour in the stock (broth). Simmer for another few minutes, then stir in the Parmesan. Remove from the heat and use a stick (immersion) blender to purée the soup coarsely, so that there are still lumps of courgette in it. Ladle into bowls, add the torn basil and chopped mint, stir in the crème fraîche and drizzle with olive oil. Serve with toasted bread and a bowl of Parmesan on the side.

Roast beetroot, goat's cheese and walnut salad

The simplest recipes are so often the best, particularly when it comes to salads, where it is tempting to add an ingredient or two too many, producing equal confusion on the plate and on the palate. Here, a handful of beetroot (beets) are roasted to earthy sweetness, before being combined with pale, creamy goat's cheese, crunchy walnuts and a tangy balsamic dressing. The contrasting bold colours, scents, textures and flavour profiles come together in this easiest of vegetarian starters (appetizers) to create a dish with powerful sensory appeal.

Preparation time: 10 minutes
Cooking time: 30–45 minutes
Serves: 2 as a starter (appetizer)

- 4 small beetroot (beets), halved
- 120 g / 4 oz mixed salad leaves (greens), washed
- 100 g / 3½ oz soft goat's cheese
- 60 g / 2¼ oz (½ cup) toasted walnuts, broken
- 1 tablespoon snipped chives
- crusty bread, to serve

For the dressing:
- 4 tablespoons extra virgin olive oil
- 2 tablespoons balsamic vinegar
- sea salt and black pepper

Preheat the oven to 170°C / 335°F / Gas Mark 3.

Wrap the beetroot (beets) together in aluminium foil and roast in the oven for 30–45 minutes until soft.

Divide the salad leaves (greens) among 4 plates. Slice the roasted beetroot and lay them over the salad leaves. Crumble the goat's cheese over the beetroot and sprinkle the broken walnuts and snipped chives on top.

To make the dressing, combine the extra virgin olive oil with the balsamic vinegar and season well. Drizzle the dressing over the salad just before serving. Serve with crusty bread on the side.

Mackerel with Romesco sauce

Romesco is a tomato-based sauce, originating from the port city of Tarragona in northeastern Spain. I like the depth of flavour sun-dried tomatoes bring to the other traditional ingredients of almonds, peppers and garlic. The gloriously punchy Romesco sauce cuts through the richness of oily fish and it is also a perfect accompaniment to chicken or lamb. Here I have paired it with mackerel, which I serve with seasonal salad leaves (greens) or a simple salad of ripe tomatoes, olives and oregano.

Preparation time: 10 minutes
Cooking time: 15–20 minutes
Serves: 4

- 180 g / 6 oz (1¼ cups) blanched almonds
- 2 cloves garlic, chopped
- 280 g / 10 oz sun-dried tomatoes in oil, chopped
- 170-g / 6-oz jar peeled red (bell) peppers, chopped
- 2 tablespoons sherry vinegar
- 1 tablespooon olive oil
- 4 fresh mackerel, scaled and gutted (cleaned)
- sea salt and black pepper

To serve:
- 4 lemon wedges, grilled
- extra virgin olive oil, for drizzling
- large bunch seasonal salad leaves (greens), washed

Slowly toast the almonds in a dry frying pan (skillet) over a low heat for 5–10 minutes until golden.

Put the toasted almonds and the chopped garlic, sun-dried tomatoes, peppers and vinegar into a blender or food processor and pulse until smooth. With the motor running, slowly drizzle in the olive oil. If the sauce is too thick, add some warm water. Transfer to a bowl and season with salt and pepper.

When you are ready to cook the fish, preheat the grill to its highest setting. Rinse the mackerel inside and out and pat dry. Slash each fish 3 or 4 times to the bone on each side and season with salt and pepper. Place on the grill rack or in a grill basket and grill for about 4 minutes on each side until cooked through.

Serve the fish on warm plates with the lemon wedges and a drizzle of extra virgin olive oil, with the romesco sauce and some salad leaves (greens) on the side.

GF

Jerusalem artichoke soup

Jerusalem artichokes are not generally appreciated. This may be due to their knobbly ugly shape, which makes them difficult to peel. I love their sweet nutty flavour, however, and their wonderful velvety texture when blended. This recipe uses Jerusalem artichokes two ways: to make a creamy smooth soup and to make crisp and golden crunchy crisps (chips) that are added as a garnish.

Preparation time: 20 minutes
Cooking time: 40 minutes
Serves: 6

- 30 g / 1 oz (2 tablespoons) unsalted butter
- 2 tablespoons olive oil
- 1 large onion, finely chopped
- 2 cloves garlic, finely chopped
- 1 sprig thyme, leaves picked, plus extra for sprinkling
- 1 kg / 2¼ lb Jerusalem artichokes, scrubbed clean and peeled
- 750 ml / 25 fl oz (3 cups) vegetable stock (broth)
- 250 ml / 8 fl oz (1 cup) milk
- 90 ml / 3 fl oz (⅓ cup) double (heavy) cream
- sea salt and black pepper
- bread, to serve
- a drizzle of truffle oil, to serve (optional)

For the artichoke crisps (chips):
- 2 Jerusalem artichokes, washed
- 1–2 tablespoons unsalted butter

Melt the butter with the olive oil in a large heavy saucepan over a medium heat. Add the onion, garlic and thyme leaves and cook for 5–10 minutes until they are softened but not coloured. Add the artichokes and cook for about 10 minutes until they are just tender. Add the stock and simmer for another 20 minutes.

Meanwhile, make the artichoke crisps (chips). Finely slice the two unpeeled artichokes with a mandoline or vegetable peeler. Put the artichoke slices and the butter in a frying pan (skillet) and fry them for a few minutes, tossing them as you do so, until they are golden and crispy.

Remove the soup from the heat, add the milk and cream and purée with a stick (immersion) blender until smooth. Season to taste with salt and pepper. Serve the soup in warm bowls with a few of the artichoke crisps on the top, a sprinkle of thyme leaves and some bread on the side. A drizzle of truffle oil will not go amiss.

Leek and Stilton tart

The natural sweetness of roasted leeks works very well with the salty pungency of creamy Stilton, especially when the two are baked together in a rich egg custard. While this tart — based on a recipe in Aaron Bertelsen's *The Great Dixter Cookbook* — is delicious eaten on a picnic, I prefer to serve it as a lunch dish during the winter months, when its two principal ingredients are at their seasonal prime — Stilton is made in the summer, but does not reach its peak until December, when it has had time to mature.

Preparation time: 10 minutes, plus minimum 1 hour chilling time
Cooking time: 1 hour 30 minutes
Serves: 6–8

- 225 g / 8 oz (1¾ cups plus 1 tablespoon) plain (all-purpose) flour, plus extra for dusting
- pinch of sea salt
- 150 g / 5 oz (1¼ sticks) unsalted chilled butter, diced
- 1 egg, separated
- 1 tablespoon iced water
- fresh green salad, to serve

For the filling:
- 2 leeks (white and light green parts), washed and sliced into 2.5-cm (1-inch) pieces
- 30 ml / 1 fl oz (2 tablespoons) olive oil
- 300 g / 10 oz rindless Stilton cheese, crumbled
- 200 g / 7 oz (¾ cup plus 1 tablespoon) crème fraîche
- 6 eggs
- 100 ml / 3½ fl oz (⅓ cup plus 1 tablespoon) milk
- sea salt and black pepper

First, make the pastry dough. Put the flour and salt into a food processor, add the butter and pulse until the mixture resembles fine breadcrumbs. Add the egg yolk and process again, then, with the motor still running, trickle in just enough cold water to bring the dough together in lumps (you may not need it all). Transfer to a large bowl and gather the pastry dough into a ball with your hands. Wrap the pastry in clingfilm (plastic wrap) and chill in the refrigerator for at least 1 hour.

Preheat the oven to 190°C / 375°F / Gas Mark 5.

Unwrap the pastry dough, knead it until it is pliable, then roll out thinly into a 26-cm (10-inch) circle on a lightly floured surface. Carefully lift the pastry dough onto the rolling pin and drape it over a loose-bottomed 23 × 4-cm (9 × 1½-inch) tart pan. Press into the sides of the pan and trim the top using a knife. Chill the pastry dough case (shell) in the refrigerator for 30 minutes. Remove from the refrigerator and prick the base with a fork, line the pastry case with greaseproof (wax) paper, fill with baking beans (pie weights) and bake 'blind' on the middle shelf of the oven for 15 minutes. Remove the paper and beans. Brush the inside of the case with the egg white, then bake for another 10 minutes until the pastry is golden brown and crisp. Remove from the oven, transfer to a cooling rack and allow to cool.

To make the filling, toss the leeks in the olive oil using your hands, then put them into a baking pan and roast in the oven until they are soft and beginning to turn brown at the edges. Arrange the crumbled Stilton inside the pastry case and cover with the leeks.

Put the crème fraîche, eggs and milk into a bowl and beat together. Pour this mixture over the leeks and season well with salt and pepper. Place the tart pan on a baking sheet and bake in the oven for 35–40 minutes until it is just set.

Take the tart out of the oven and carefully remove the outer ring. Return the tart to the oven for 5 minutes to allow the sides to crisp up. Remove from the oven and serve with a fresh green salad.

Ribollita

This is a robust Tuscan soup, made with seasonal vegetables, beans, bread and olive oil. The Italian word ribollita means 'reboiled', referencing the fact that this was a dish historically made from leftovers. The recipe comes from the tradition of *la cucina povera*, meaning 'the cooking of the poor', which is rooted in the necessary discipline of making the most both of whatever is to hand in the kitchen and what is cheaply available in the market on any given day. This is inspired by the River Café recipe and makes a large quantity, as I like to serve ribollita as a main meal. The chicken stock (broth) can easily be replaced with a vegetable alternative to make this a vegetarian dish.

Preparation time: 20 minutes, plus overnight soaking
Cooking time: 2 hours 20 minutes
Serves: 6

- 200 g / 7 oz (1 cup) dried cannellini beans
- 1 tablespoon bicarbonate of soda (baking soda)
- 4 tablespoons olive oil
- 4 cloves garlic, chopped
- 400 g / 14 oz carrots, peeled and chopped
- 1 whole head celery, trimmed and chopped
- 4 onions, chopped
- 2 leeks, trimmed and sliced (white parts only)
- 1 bay leaf
- 1 sprig thyme
- large handful flat-leaf parsley, leaves chopped
- 2 × 400-g / 14-oz cans plum tomatoes, drained of their juices and chopped
- 1 kg / 2¼ lb cavolo nero (Tuscan kale), stalks removed and leaves coarsely chopped
- 250 ml / 8 fl oz (1 cup) chicken stock (broth), plus extra if needed
- 2 stale ciabatta loaves, torn into pieces
- 45 ml / 1½ fl oz (3 tablespoons) extra virgin olive oil
- sea salt and black pepper

Soak the beans overnight in a generous amount of water to which you have added the bicarbonate of soda (baking soda). The following day, drain the beans thoroughly and place them in a saucepan. Cover with cold water, bring to the boil and simmer for 10 minutes. Drain, cover again with fresh water and continue to simmer for about 40 minutes until the beans are tender. Drain and set aside.

Heat the oil in a large saucepan over a medium heat, add the garlic, carrot, celery, onion, leek, bay leaf, thyme and parsley and fry for 25 minutes. Add the tomatoes and continue to cook over a low heat for another 25 minutes before adding the cavolo nero (Tuscan kale), half the cooked cannellini beans and the stock (broth). Let it simmer for 30–40 minutes, stirring occasionally.

Put the remaining beans into a food processor, process until smooth and add to the pan. Add the bread and extra virgin olive oil and season to taste. Stir and if the soup is too thick, add some more stock and serve.

Chicken, leek and ham pie

A generous pie with a burnished pastry top, the preparation of which fills the house with comforting aromas, is a wonderfully homely dish to serve in winter. I like to use thighs rather than breasts of chicken for this recipe, because the leg meat is more tender and also has a deeper flavour.

Preparation time: 20 minutes
Cooking time: 1 hour 20 minutes
Serves: 4

- 10 chicken thighs (skin on, bone in)
- 3 tablespoons extra virgin olive oil
- 4 sprigs thyme
- 2 strips lemon peel
- 8 cloves garlic, peeled
- 4 tablespoons plain (all-purpose) flour, plus extra for dusting
- 140 ml / 4½ fl oz (⅔ cup) white wine
- 225 ml / 8 fl oz (¾ cup plus 2 tablespoons) chicken stock (broth)
- 100 ml / 3½ fl oz (⅓ cup plus 1 tablespoon) double (heavy) cream
- 15 g / ½ oz (1 tablespoon) unsalted butter
- 4 leeks, trimmed and cut into 10-cm (4-inch) slices
- 3 thick slices ham, cut into strips
- 450 g / 1 lb all-butter puff pastry
- 1 egg
- 1–2 teaspoons milk
- sea salt and black pepper

Season the chicken thighs well. Heat the olive oil in a large sauté pan over a medium heat, add the chicken thighs, thyme sprigs and lemon peel and fry for about 5 minutes, turning them until they begin to colour. Add the garlic towards the end so that it softens without changing colour. Sprinkle the flour over the chicken, ensuring that all sides are coated. Stir in the wine and cook for a minute before adding the chicken stock (broth) and cream and some salt and pepper. Bring to a simmer, cover and cook gently for 25 minutes.

While the chicken is cooking, melt the butter in a frying pan (skillet) over a medium heat and add the leeks. Cook for about 5 minutes until soft but not browned.

Preheat the oven to 220°C / 425°F / Gas Mark 7.

Remove the skin and bones from the chicken, cut the meat into shreds and put into a 1.7-litre / 57-fl oz (7¼-cup) pie dish with the sauce from the sauté pan. Remove and discard the lemon zest and thyme sprigs. Add the cooked leeks and ham to the chicken.

Roll out the puff pastry to about 5 mm (¼ inch) thick on a lightly floured surface and drape over the pie dish, leaving a 1-cm (½-inch) overhang to allow for shrinkage. Press the edges of the pastry onto the rim of the dish with your thumb or crimp with a fork.

Using a sharp knife make a few cuts in the pastry to allow the steam to escape. Beat the egg and milk together in a small bowl to make an egg wash. Brush this all over the pastry, then bake the pie in the oven for 45–50 minutes until the pastry is crisp and golden. Remove from the oven and serve.

Slow cooked shoulder of lamb

This method of preparing lamb produces meat that melts in the mouth. The shoulder is cooked very slowly over a period of hours, filling the kitchen with spicy smells until the meat literally falls off the bone when it is pulled with a fork. Because the joint requires minimal attention while it is cooking — just a little occasional basting — this is a perfect dish to prepare on a day when there are other demands on your time. Serve with the Rice, Puy lentils and caramelized shallots (page 252).

Preparation time: 20 minutes, plus overnight marinating
Cooking time: 5 hours, plus 25 minutes resting time
Serves: 6

- 2 kg / 4½ lb lamb shoulder
- 4 onions, thickly sliced

For the marinade:
- ½ teaspoon cumin seeds
- ½ teaspoon coriander seeds
- 2 shallots, halved
- 3 cloves garlic
- 2 tomatoes, coarsely chopped
- 3 canned anchovy fillets in oil
- 1½ tablespoons rosemary needles or thyme leaves
- handful mint, leaves chopped
- 80 ml / 2¾ fl oz (5½ tablespoons) white wine
- 60 ml / 2 fl oz (4 tablespoons) olive oil
- 1 tablespoon soft light brown sugar
- grated zest and juice of 1 lemon

GF

To make the marinade, first toast the cumin and coriander seeds in a dry frying pan (skillet) over a low heat until fragrant, then transfer to a food processor with all the remaining marinade ingredients and process until coarsely blended.

Make shallow cuts all over the lamb shoulder with a knife. Lay the lamb in a large roasting pan and coat with the marinade, rubbing it into the flesh. Cover with clingfilm (plastic wrap) and leave in the refrigerator overnight. Remove the joint from the refrigerator an hour or two before cooking.

Preheat the oven to 160°C / 325°F / Gas Mark 3.

Lay the sliced onions in a deep roasting pan, unwrap the lamb and place it on top. Cover the pan with aluminium foil and roast in the oven for 5 hours, basting the meat every now and then. Take the pan from the oven, transfer the lamb shoulder — still covered in foil — to a chopping (cutting) board and allow it to rest for 25 minutes. Return the pan with the onions and marinating juices to the still-warm oven.

Remove the foil and pull apart the meat of the lamb using two forks. Skim away any fat from the roasting juices then serve with the lamb and warm, roasted onions.

Poached fish with ginger broth

This fresh and elegant broth is light but satisfying and also quick to prepare. I buy fish stock from my local fishmonger, but it is available in many supermarkets and you can also make your own.

Preparation time: 10 minutes
Cooking time: 10 minutes
Serves: 2

- 3-cm (1¼-inch) piece of fresh ginger, peeled and finely chopped
- 2 cloves garlic, finely chopped
- 3 spring onions (scallions), thinly sliced
- 750 ml / 25 fl oz (3 cups) fish stock (broth)
- 50 g / 2 oz tenderstem broccoli (broccolini), trimmed and halved
- 2 fillets any white fish (such as cod) or salmon
- 2 pak choi (bok choy)
- ½ teaspoon white or black sesame seeds, toasted
- a few coriander (cilantro) leaves
- a few thin slices of fresh red chilli (chile)
- sea salt and black pepper

Put the ginger, garlic and spring onions (scallions) into a large sauté pan with a lid and pour over the stock (broth). Place over a medium heat and simmer for about 5 minutes to release the flavours of the aromatics into the stock.

Add the broccoli (broccolini) and fish to the pan and poach gently with the lid on for 5 minutes, taking care not to overcook the fish. Gently stir the pak choi (bok choy) into the broth and allow to wilt. Remove the fish and place in large bowls, then pour over the broth and vegetables. Sprinkle with the sesame seeds, coriander (cilantro) and fresh chilli (chile) and season to taste.

GF

Saffron chicken tagine with dried fruits

This is the most famous of all Moroccan dishes, traditionally cooked slowly in an earthenware tagine pot over an open fire. Any meat can be used, but lamb or chicken are the most commonly found versions. If, like me, you do not own a tagine pot, any wide, shallow pot with a tight-fitting lid will work equally well. This is a dish you can prepare the day before to allow the spices to infuse and intensify. I serve it with bread, rice or couscous to mop up the juices. It is gluten free if you serve it with rice.

—

Preparation time: 20 minutes
Cooking time: 1 hour 25 minutes
Serves: 6

- 1 tablespoon olive oil
- 3 onions, coarsely chopped
- 4 cloves garlic, coarsely chopped
- 3 tablespoons ras-el-hanout
- 1 teaspoon ground cumin seeds
- 1 teaspoon ground coriander
- 1 teaspoon ground ginger
- 1 large organic free-range chicken (about 1.5 kg / 3¼ lb), jointed
- 2 preserved lemons, chopped
- 3 pinches of saffron strands steeped in 1 tablespoon of boiling water for 20 minutes
- 200 ml / 7 fl oz (¾ cup plus 1 tablespoon) chicken stock (broth)
- 50 g / 2 oz (⅓ cup) Iranian sultanas (golden raisins) or others if these are not available
- 50 g / 2 oz (⅓ cup) stoned (pitted) and coarsely chopped soft prunes
- 50 g / 2 oz (⅓ cup) dried apricots
- 100 g / 3½ oz (1 cup) stoned (pitted) green olives
- sea salt and black pepper

To serve:
- 50 g / 2 oz (½ cup) flaked (slivered) almonds, toasted
- large handful chopped coriander (cilantro), to garnish
- Flatbreads (page 099), rice or couscous

Heat the olive oil in a large, heavy saucepan or casserole dish over a medium heat, add the onions and garlic and sauté for about 5 minutes until soft and translucent. Add all the dry spices and sauté for another 5 minutes, then add the chicken pieces and stir to coat them in the onions and spices. Allow the chicken pieces to brown skin side down, turning the pieces after about 5 minutes to brown the other side. Stir in the preserved lemons and the saffron and steeping water. Pour in the stock (broth), cover and cook over a low heat for 1 hour.

While the chicken is cooking, soak the sultanas (golden raisins) in boiling water in a small heatproof bowl. Put the rest of the dried fruit into a small saucepan, cover with water and bring to the boil. Drain the fruit and stir it into the chicken with the olives. Cook for another 5 minutes and season well with salt and pepper.

Sprinkle the flaked (slivered) almonds and chopped coriander (cilantro) on top of the chicken and serve with flatbreads, rice or couscous to absorb the juices.

Pappardelle with venison, mushrooms and carrots

Venison haunch is delicious roasted until the meat is still pink in the middle, but also rewards from slower cooking, which brings out its rich flavours and ensures the meat is meltingly tender – the diet and exercise of wild deer means that venison does not have the marbling of fat typical of domestically reared animals, which can make it vulnerable to toughness. This is a hearty, comforting dish. It is perfectly complemented by the woodiness of mushrooms and the pasta, which takes up the juices.

Preparation time: 30 minutes, plus overnight marinating
Cooking time: 3 hours
Serves: 6

- 1 kg / 2¼ lb venison haunch, trimmed and diced
- 200 ml / 7 fl oz (¾ cup plus 1 tablespoon) red wine
- 1 clove garlic, crushed
- olive oil, for frying
- 60 g / 2 oz smoked pancetta, diced
- 2 onions, finely chopped
- 2 carrots, trimmed, peeled and cubed
- 3 tablespoons tomato purée (paste)
- 1 sprig thyme
- 1 sprig rosemary
- 1 bay leaf
- 25 g / ¾ oz (2 tablespoons) plain (all-purpose) flour
- 1.2 litres / 40 fl oz (5 cups) chicken stock (broth)
- 400 g / 14 oz dried pappardelle pasta
- 450 g / 1 lb seasonal wild mushrooms of choice, sliced
- 1 bunch flat-leaf parsley, leaves finely chopped
- sea salt and black pepper
- 50 g / 2 oz Parmesan cheese, finely grated, to serve

The day before you want to serve this dish, put the diced venison into a large nonreactive container, add the wine and crushed clove of garlic, cover and place in the refrigerator, turning the meat once or twice.

The next day, preheat the oven to 160°C / 325°F / Gas Mark 3. Drain the venison and pat dry. Keep the marinade (discarding the garlic) and set aside.

Heat a drizzle of olive oil in a frying pan (skillet) over a medium heat and sear the venison in batches, cooking each batch for a few minutes until browned. Transfer the browned meat to a lidded casserole dish with a slotted spoon. Once all the meat is browned, add the diced pancetta to the same frying pan and fry until it has rendered most of its fat and started to become crispy, then remove and set aside. Add the onion to the pan and cook for 5–10 minutes until softened and lightly golden, then add the carrot, tomato purée (paste), thyme, rosemary, bay leaf and flour and return the pancetta to the pan. Cook for a couple of minutes, then pour in the reserved marinade, little by little, stirring and letting it bubble and reduce. Add the stock (broth), stirring to avoid any lumps, then pour it over the venison in the casserole. Cover and transfer to the oven for about 2½ hours, or until the venison is soft and tender. Season with salt and pepper to taste.

Cook the pasta in a large saucepan of salted boiling water according to the instructions on the package, then drain.

Meanwhile, heat a little oil in a frying pan over a medium heat, add the mushrooms and sauté for 10–15 minutes until they have released their water, softened and are slightly crisped at the edges. Add the mushrooms to the venison, stir in the pasta, sprinkle with chopped parsley and serve straight away, with the grated Parmesan on the side.

Kedgeree

The combination of smoked fish, eggs and rice fragrant with herbs and spices makes this a wonderful option for brunch or for a light lunch or supper. The origins of the Anglo-Indian recipe are said to lie in a dish called *kichdi*, a combination of spiced lentils, ginger, rice and fried onions eaten across India that dates back to the fourteenth century and which is also traditionally the first solid food given to babies.

Preparation time: 15 minutes
Cooking time: 35 minutes
Serves: 6

- 300 g / 10 oz undyed smoked haddock fillet, skin on
- 2 bay leaves
- 300 ml / 10 fl oz (1¼ cups) milk
- 6 eggs
- chopped flat-leaf parsley, to taste
- chopped coriander (cilantro), to taste
- 1 tablespoon butter
- finely sliced spring onions (scallions), to taste

For the rice:
- 2 tablespoons vegetable oil
- 1 onion, finely chopped
- 2 teaspoons ground coriander
- 2 teaspoons ground turmeric
- 2 teaspoons curry powder
- 350 g / 12 oz (1¾ cups) long-grain white rice, rinsed
- sea salt and black pepper

Place the haddock and bay leaves in a large frying pan (skillet) and cover with the milk. Place over a medium heat and bring to the boil, then reduce the heat and simmer for about 10 minutes until the fish is cooked and the flesh flakes easily. Remove from the heat, remove the haddock from the milk (discard the milk and bay leaves) and allow the haddock to cool before removing the skin and flaking the fish into pieces.

To cook the rice, heat the oil in a large saucepan with a lid over a medium–low heat, add the onion and cook gently for a few minutes until it is soft and translucent. Add the ground coriander, ground turmeric and curry powder, season with salt and pepper and continue to fry for about 4 minutes, being careful not to let the spices burn. Add the rinsed rice and stir in well, to coat the grains in the oil and spice, then pour in 600 ml / 20 fl oz (2½ cups) water and bring to the boil. Reduce the heat, cover and simmer for about 10 minutes, or until the rice is cooked and all the water has been absorbed. Remove from the heat, put the lid on and leave for 15 minutes.

While the rice is standing, put the eggs into a saucepan, cover with cold water, bring to the boil, then reduce the heat and simmer for 4–5 minutes (depending on how runny you want the yolks to be). Plunge into cold water, and as soon as they are cool enough to handle, peel off the shells and cut each egg in quarters.

Mix the fish and rice together. Add the parsley and coriander (cilantro), stir in the butter, then transfer to plates or bowls and lay the boiled eggs on the top, cut side up. Sprinkle with more parsley and some spring onions (scallions) and serve.

GF

Hasselback potatoes

Hasselback potatoes are a Swedish variation on the traditional roast potato, the name of the dish deriving from the Stockholm restaurant — Hasselbacken — where it was first served. Each potato is cut into very thin slices that stop just short of the base. These slices fan out slightly during cooking, creating potatoes with crispy edges and soft, creamy middles, thereby combining the best characteristics of both roasties and mashed potatoes.

Preparation time: 20 minutes
Cooking time: 1 hour 10 minutes
Serves: 6

- maincrop (main-season) floury potatoes, peeled
- 40 g / 1½ oz (3¼ tablespoons) butter
- 90 ml / 3 fl oz (6 tablespoons) groundnut (peanut) oil
- handful chopped herbs, such as rosemary, thyme or chives
- sea salt and black pepper

Preheat the oven to 200°C / 400°F / Gas Mark 6.

In order to slice the potato and leave the bottom intact, I rest a pair of chopsticks on either side of the potato and use a sharp knife to make a series of cuts, 3 mm (⅛ inch) apart. The chopsticks prevent the blade from slicing all the way through.

Melt the butter with the oil in a saucepan over a low heat. Put the potatoes into a roasting dish, gently fan out the slices and spoon over the fat. Season generously with salt and pepper and bake in the oven for about 1 hour and 10 minutes, depending on the size of the potatoes. About 10 minutes before removing them from the oven, sprinkle over the chopped herbs.

GF

Nut loaf

Straightforward to prepare, this nut loaf is a hearty and nutritious vegetarian meal, with the mushrooms and fresh breadcrumbs helping to bring the other ingredients together, ensuring that the loaf is neither too dense nor too dry, without detracting from the primacy of the cashews. I usually serve the loaf accompanied by just a simple dressed green salad. From time to time I also make this recipe as an alternative to my usual stuffing for roast chicken, which always goes down very well with the family.

Preparation time: 20 minutes
Cooking time: 1 hour
Serves: 6–8

- 400 g / 14 oz (3 cups) cashews
- 100 g / 3½ oz (7 tablespoons) butter, plus extra for greasing
- 4 small red onions, finely chopped
- 4 cloves garlic, crushed
- 3–4 sprigs thyme, leaves only
- 600 g / 1 lb 5 oz portobello or chestnut (cremini) mushrooms, coarsely chopped
- 2 bunches flat-leaf parsley, finely chopped
- 45 ml / 1½ fl oz (3 tablespoons) soy sauce
- 150 g / 5 oz (3 cups) fresh white breadcrumbs
- salad leaves (greens), to serve

Preheat the oven to 180°C / 350°F / Gas Mark 4 and grease a 22-cm (8½-inch) loaf pan with butter and line with greaseproof (wax) paper.

Put the cashews into the roasting pan and roast in the oven for 5–10 minutes until toasted and lightly browned. Remove from the oven, leave to cool, then put them into a plastic food bag and crush with a rolling pin so that they are still coarse.

Melt the butter in a large frying pan (skillet) over a medium–low heat, add the onions and garlic and sauté for about 5 minutes until soft and translucent. Add the thyme and mushrooms and cook over a medium heat for about 10 minutes until the mushrooms are soft. Lower the heat and add the cashews, chopped parsley, soy sauce and breadcrumbs and cook for a few minutes before transferring to the lined loaf pan. Roast in the oven for 45 minutes until it is firm when pressed gently. Remove from the oven, leave to cool, then turn the pan upside down and gently ease the loaf out. Serve with salad leaves (greens).

VG

Rice, Puy lentils and caramelized shallots

This is a version of the classic Arabic dish, *mujadara*. Recipes vary from country to country and family to family, but it is essentially a combination of tender lentils and rice, garnished with crispy shallots, to which herbs and spices may be added, but which in its most pared-back iterations is seasoned only with salt and pepper. Satisfying, flavoursome and suitable for vegetarians and vegans, *mujadara* can stand alone as a meal in itself or be served alongside roasted lamb or chicken to absorb the meat juices.

Preparation time: 25 minutes
Cooking time: 35 minutes
Serves: 6

- 3 cloves garlic, crushed
- 1 bay leaf
- 1 tablespoon ground cumin
- 1 teaspoon Lebanese 7-spice blend (optional)
- 1 cinnamon stick
- pinch of sea salt
- pinch of black pepper
- 200 g / 7 oz (1 cup) basmati rice, rinsed and drained
- 95 g / 3¼ oz (½ cup) Puy (green) lentils, rinsed and drained
- 3 tablespoons extra virgin olive oil
- 4 shallots, sliced into fine rings
- 5 spring onions (scallions), trimmed and finely chopped
- bunch coriander (cilantro), chopped

Put the garlic, bay leaf, cumin, Lebanese 7-spice blend (if using), cinnamon stick, salt and pepper into a large heavy saucepan. Add 1.5 litres / 50 fl oz (5 cups) water and bring to the boil over a medium heat. Once it's boiling, add the rice and reduce the heat a little. Cover and simmer for 10 minutes. Stir in the lentils and continue to cook for another 10–15 minutes until all the liquid is absorbed and the rice and lentils are tender.

While the rice and lentils are cooking, heat the olive oil in a large frying pan (skillet) over a medium–low heat, add the shallot and cook for about 15 minutes until they are deeply caramelized and starting to crispen up. Remove from the heat and allow to cool.

Drain the rice and lentils of any excess water, remove and discard the bay leaf and cinnamon stick and return the rice to the saucepan. Add about three-quarters of the shallot and all the spring onions (scallions) to the rice and lentils and stir in gently. Transfer to a large serving bowl. Sprinkle the remaining shallot and coriander (cilantro) on the top and serve warm.

Lemon tart

This tart is relatively easy to make and produces a wonderful combination of sweet and sour. The filling needs to be thick and light, the pastry fine and crumbly.

Preparation time: 10 minutes, plus 1 hour chilling time for the pastry
Cooking time: 1 hour 30 minutes
Serves: 6–8

- 250 g / 9 oz (2 cups) plain (all-purpose) flour, plus extra for dusting
- 125 g / 4½ oz (1⅛ sticks) unsalted butter, well chilled, cut into small cubes
- 1 tablespoon caster (superfine) sugar
- 1 teaspoon vanilla extract
- 1 egg yolk
- a little iced water
- double (heavy) cream, whipped, or crème fraîche, to serve (optional)

For the filling:
- 5 eggs
- 175 g / 6 oz (¾ cup plus 2 tablespoons) caster (superfine) sugar
- 250 ml / 8 fl oz (1 cup) double (heavy) cream
- grated zest and juice of 4 lemons

VG

To make the pastry dough, tip the flour into a food processor, add the butter, sugar and vanilla extract and pulse until the mixture has the consistency of coarse breadcrumbs. Add the egg yolk and 1 tablespoon of iced water and pulse again until the pastry dough forms a ball, adding a little more water if necessary. Wrap the pastry dough in clingfilm (plastic wrap) and leave to rest in the refrigerator for 30 minutes.

Unwrap the chilled pastry dough, knead it until it is pliable, then roll it out on a lightly floured work counter into a round about 3 mm (⅛ inch) thick. Carefully lift the pastry onto the rolling pin and drape it over a 25-cm (10-inch) fluted shallow tart pan, being careful not to stretch the dough. Press the pastry gently into the fluted sides, but don't trim it around the top — it should overhang the edges of the pan to allow for shrinkage. Prick the base with a fork and chill the pastry case (shell) for 30 minutes.

Preheat the oven to 180°C / 350°F / Gas Mark 4. Remove the pastry case from the refrigerator, line it with greaseproof (wax) paper and fill it with baking beans (pie weights). Bake 'blind' on the middle shelf of the oven for 25 minutes. Remove the paper and beans and bake for another 10 minutes until the pastry case is golden brown and crisp. Remove from the oven, transfer to a cooling rack and leave to cool completely.

To make the filling, break the eggs into a bowl and whisk gently. Add the sugar and whisk again, then add the cream and lemon juice and zest and whisk to combine.

Reduce the oven temperature to 100°C / 225°F / Gas Mark ¼. When the pastry has cooled, carefully pour in the lemon filling to reach the top of the tart and bake in the oven for about 1 hour until it has just set. Serve with whipped cream or crème fraiche, if you like.

Sticky toffee pudding

This is a rich, wildly indulgent dessert, with black treacle (molasses) bringing its unmistakable intensity and notes of spice. The fact that it is eaten warm makes it an ideal pudding for the colder months, with the added advantage that it can be prepared in advance and warmed up prior to serving. To accompany, I prefer the slightly more pronounced flavour of crème fraîche to the dish's traditional partners of double (heavy) cream, vanilla ice cream or custard.

Preparation time: 30 minutes
Cooking time: 30 minutes
Serves: 8–10

- 175 g / 6 oz (1 cup plus 3 tablespoons) coarsely chopped dried stoned (pitted) dates
- 175 ml / 6 fl oz (¾ cup) boiling water
- 140 g / 4¾ oz (1 cup plus 2 tablespoons) plain (all-purpose) flour
- 2 teaspoons baking powder
- 2 tablespoons black treacle (molasses)
- 75 g / 2¾ oz (5 tablespoons) unsalted butter, softened and cubed, plus extra for greasing
- 3 tablespoons light muscovado sugar
- 2 eggs
- crème fraîche, to serve

For the sauce:
- 75 g / 5 oz (1¼ sticks) unsalted butter, softened and cubed
- ½ tablespoon black treacle (molasses)
- 150 g / 5 oz (⅓ cup) dark muscovado sugar
- 1 teaspoon vanilla extract
- 100 ml / 3½ fl oz (⅓ cup plus 1 tablespoon) double (heavy) cream

Put the chopped dates into a heatproof bowl, pour over the boiling water and leave to soak for 10 minutes.

Preheat the oven to 180°C / 350°F / Gas Mark 4 and lightly grease a 23-cm (9-inch) loaf pan.

In a bowl, mix together the flour and baking powder. Set aside. Put the black treacle (molasses) and butter into the bowl of a stand mixer fitted with a whisk attachment, or in a bowl with a handheld electric whisk and cream until well combined, then add the sugar and mix again until there are no lumps. Beat in the eggs, one at a time. Fold in the flour and baking powder, and mix until smooth. Stir in the dates and their soaking liquid. Scrape the batter into the prepared pan and bake in the oven for 30 minutes or until the cake is firm and a skewer inserted into the middle of the cake comes out clean.

While the pudding is baking, prepare the sauce. Put the butter into a heavy saucepan and melt over a low heat. Add the treacle, sugar and vanilla extract and stir gently until the sugar has dissolved. Stir in the cream, turn up the heat and cook until the sauce starts to bubble, then remove from the heat.

Remove the cake from the oven, prick the top of the cake all over with a fork, pour some of the sauce over it and allow it to soak in. Serve the cake with crème fraîche and the remaining sauce.

VG

Pear tatin

Autumn (fall) and winter — when there is a glut of pears on the trees in the garden and in the shops — are ideal times to make this variation of the classic French upside-down dessert. The poached orchard fruit, aromatic with ginger, cinnamon and its own heady scent, is baked in caramel, under crisp puff pastry. When the tatin is turned out, the pear halves are sticky with spiced, syrupy juices. Rather than presented searingly hot, direct from the oven, this dish is best served just warm, with cream, crème fraîche or ice cream. What could be nicer?

Preparation time: 10 minutes
Cooking time: 40–60 minutes
Serves: 6

- 4 regular or 3 large pears, peeled, cored and halved
- 1 cinnamon stick
- knob of fresh ginger, peeled
- ½ lemon, for squeezing
- 125 g / 4½ oz (½ cup plus 2 tablespoons) caster (superfine) sugar
- 40 g / 1½ oz (2¾ tablespoons) cold unsalted butter, cubed
- 320 g / 11¼ oz ready-rolled all-butter puff pastry
- double (heavy) cream, ice cream or crème fraîche, to serve

VG

Preheat the oven to 200°C / 400°F / Gas Mark 6.

Put the peeled pear halves into a saucepan with the cinnamon stick and knob of ginger, squeeze in the lemon juice and cover with water. Poach gently over a low heat for 10–15 minutes until the pears begin to soften but are still firm. Remove from the heat and leave in the water to continue to cook and take on the flavours of the spices.

Put a 21-cm (8¼-inch) diameter heavy ovenproof frying pan (skillet) on the hob (stove) over a medium heat. Add the sugar, reduce the heat to low and allow it to cook until it is a golden caramel colour, stirring constantly. Add the butter, remove from the heat and continue to stir.

Remove the pears from the poaching water with a slotted spoon. Now it's time to assemble the tarte tatin. Carefully lay the pears cut side down into the caramel in a nice shape. Allow to cool a little.

Unroll the pastry dough (it should be about 5 mm / ¼ inch thick) and cut a disc slightly larger than the ovenproof pan (about 24 cm / 9½ inches). Carefully drape the pastry on top of the pears and caramel and tuck it around the sides of the pan, enclosing the pears. Using a fork, prick the pastry to allow the steam to escape and then bake in the oven for 30–40 minutes until the pastry is golden, crisp and puffed up. Remove from the oven, allow to cool a little, then run a knife around the edge to loosen the pastry from the edges of the pan. Place a large plate over the top of the pan and carefully flip over and turn the tarte tatin out. Serve warm with double (heavy) cream, ice cream or crème fraîche.

Ginger Florentines

This recipe is a refined twist on the traditional Florentine, by the inspirational chef Sally Clarke. Studded with almonds, hazelnuts, crystallized ginger and sultanas (golden raisins) they are a delicious nutty treat to serve alongside a fresh fruit salad or simply to eat on their own.

Preparation time: 10 minutes
Cooking time: 20 minutes
Makes: 12 florentines

- 75 g / 2¾ oz (½ cup) hazelnuts
- 35 g / 1¼ oz (2½ tablespoons) unsalted butter
- 90 ml / 3 fl oz (6 tablespoons) double (heavy) cream
- 60 g / 2 oz (¼ cup) caster (superfine) sugar
- 100 g / 3½ oz (1 cup) flaked (slivered) almonds
- 55 g / 2 oz crystallized ginger, coarsely chopped
- 30 g / 1 oz (3½ tablespoons) sultanas (golden raisins)
- 1 teaspoon plain (all-purpose) flour

Preheat the oven to 180°C / 350°F / Gas Mark 4 and line a baking sheet with baking (parchment) paper.

Spread out the hazelnuts on a baking sheet and roast in the oven for 5–10 minutes until the skins start to flake away. Remove from the oven and leave to cool, then rub gently in a clean cloth. Discard the skins and coarsely chop the nuts.

Slowly bring the butter, cream and sugar to the boil in a saucepan. Add the remaining ingredients, mixing gently but thoroughly.

Using a tablespoon, spoon out 12 mounds onto the lined baking sheet, leaving plenty of space for the Florentines to expand and bake in the oven for 8–10 minutes until golden. Remove from the oven, allow to cool and serve.

VG

Profiteroles

This was one of my mother's favourite dinner party desserts in South Africa in the 1970s. What could be more enticing than hollow spheres of crisp choux pastry, filled with sweetened vanilla-scented cream and covered in warm chocolate? Once you have poured the sauce over the profiteroles, they should be served immediately.

—

Preparation time: 30 minutes
Cooking time: 25 minutes
Makes: about 24

- 50 g / 2 oz (3½ tablespoons) unsalted butter, cubed
- 1 tablespoon caster (superfine) sugar
- 80 g / 3 oz (½ cup plus 2 tablespoons) white strong (bread) flour, sifted
- pinch of fine salt
- 2 eggs, lightly beaten

For the cream filling:
- 325 ml / 11 fl oz (1⅓ cups) double (heavy) cream
- 1 tablespoon caster (superfine) sugar
- 3–4 drops of vanilla extract

For the chocolate sauce:
- 90 g / 3¼ oz (⅓ cup plus 2 tablespoons) caster (superfine) sugar
- 180 g / 6 oz dark (semisweet) chocolate (70% cocoa solids), chopped into small pieces

Preheat the oven to 200°C / 400°F / Gas Mark 6.

To make the profiteroles, put the butter and caster (superfine) sugar into a heavy-bottom saucepan and add 150 ml / 5 fl oz (⅔ cup) water. Melt over a low heat, then bring to the boil. Remove the pan from the heat, tip in all the flour and salt, then beat it in vigorously with a wooden spoon for a minute or two until the dough forms a ball and starts to come away from the sides of the pan. Return the pan to a low heat for 2–3 minutes. Let it cool for 5 minutes whilst continuing to beat it, then beat in the eggs, little by little, with a fork until you have a smooth paste.

Spray two non-stick baking sheets with a little cold water. Using a spoon or a piping (pastry) bag, place small amounts of the mixture onto the sheets, well spaced out, then bake in the oven for about 20 minutes until risen and lightly golden. Remove the profiteroles from the oven and immediately pierce the side of each bun with a small knife to release the steam. Cool on a wire rack.

To make the filling, lightly whisk the cream in a bowl, then fold in the sugar and vanilla extract to combine.

For the chocolate sauce, put the sugar and 100 ml / 3½ fl oz (⅓ cup plus 1 tablespoon) water into a small saucepan and bring to the boil to make a syrup. Reduce the heat to a simmer and melt the chocolate in a heatproof bowl set over the pan, stirring occasionally. Take the pan off the heat, pour the syrup mixture into the chocolate in the bowl and stir until smooth and well combined.

Cut each profiterole in half and fill with the cream. Pile them up on a plate and chill to prevent them from going soggy. Allow the chocolate sauce to cool, before drizzling it over the pile of profiteroles. Serve straight away.

VG

All butter is salted, unless otherwise specified.
All milk is full-fat (whole) milk, unless otherwise specified.
All eggs are organic and large (US extra-large), unless otherwise specified.
All pepper is freshly ground black pepper, unless otherwise specified.
All sugar is organic caster (superfine) sugar, unless otherwise specified.

Individual vegetables and fruits, such as carrots and apples, are assumed to be medium, unless otherwise specified.

Exercise a high level of caution when following recipes involving any potentially hazardous activity, including the use of high temperatures, open flames and when deep-frying. In particular, when deep-frying add food carefully to avoid splashing, wear long sleeves and never leave the pan unattended.

Cooking times are for guidance only. If using a fan (convection) oven, follow the manufacturer's instructions concerning the oven temperatures.

Some recipes include lightly cooked eggs, meat and fish, and fermented products. These should be avoided by the elderly, infants, pregnant women, convalescents and anyone with an impaired immune system.

Exercise caution when making fermented products, ensuring all equipment is spotlessly clean, and seek expert advice if in any doubt.

All herbs, shoots, flowers, berries, seeds and vegetables should be picked fresh from a clean source. Exercise caution when foraging for ingredients. Any foraged ingredients should only be eaten if an expert has deemed them safe to eat.

When no quantity is specified, for example of oils, salts and herbs used for finishing dishes, quantities are discretionary and flexible.

All spoon and cup measurements are level, unless otherwise stated.
1 teaspoon = 5 ml; 1 tablespoon = 15 ml. Australian standard tablespoons are 20 ml, so Australian readers are advised to use 3 teaspoons in place of 1 tablespoon when measuring small quantities.

Recipes that are vegetarian (VG), vegan (VE) or gluten free (GF) are marked at the bottom of the relevant page.

Catherine Pawson grew up in a large family in Johannesburg, South Africa. She studied at the Inchbald School of Design in London and worked at Colefax & Fowler before embarking on a long-term partnership with fellow interiors specialist Juliet Byrne. She continues to work as an interior designer and decorator.

John Pawson grew up in an equally large family on the edge of the Yorkshire Moors in the north of England and established his architectural design practice in London in 1981. Notable collaborators over the years have included Calvin Klein, Ian Schrager and the choreographer Wayne McGregor, with diverse commissions ranging from the Cistercian Abbey of Nový Dvůr in the Czech Republic, a lake crossing within Kew's Royal Botanic Gardens and the interior renovation of the Design Museum's new permanent home in west London. In 2019 he was appointed CBE, for services to architecture and design.

John and Catherine have three grown-up children and a grandson and divide their time between their London house, where they have lived for a little over two decades and Home Farm on the edge of a hamlet in the Cotswolds.

Phaidon Press Limited
2 Cooperage Yard
London E15 2QR

Phaidon Press Inc.
65 Bleecker Street
New York, NY 10012

phaidon.com

We would like to thank Gilbert McCarragher for his photography; Alison Morris for her help with the words; Nicholas Barba for designing the book; Philip McMullen for testing the recipes and for his unfailingly calm presence in the kitchen; Phaidon Press's publisher Emilia Terragni and our project editor, Sophie Hodgkin; our brilliant cooking assistants, Eva Astor and Clarissa Berning; and Clementine Crawford, Phoebe Greenwood and Sarah Miller for their invaluable advice.

The majority of the items of cookware, tableware, homeware, furniture, lighting and textiles featured in *Home Farm Cooking* — and in regular service at Home Farm — are John Pawson designs. They have been developed and manufactured by companies with whom John's working relationship is, in some cases, of many years standing, including 1882 Ltd, Benchmark, Demeyere, Salvatori, Swarovski, Teixidors, Tekla, Viccarbe, Wästberg, When Objects Work and WonderGlass.

—

First published 2021

ISBN 978 1 83866 126 7
(trade edition)

ISBN 978 1 83866 287 5
(signed edition)

A CIP catalogue record for this book is available from the British Library and the Library of Congress.

Printed in China

Commissioning Editor:
Emilia Terragni

Project Editor:
Sophie Hodgkin

Production Controller:
Jane Harman

Design:
Nicholas Barba

Photography:
Gilbert McCarragher

Additional Photography:
John Pawson 025, 026, 029 (top), 033, 034 (top), 086, 094, 205, 209, 210/211, 213 and 214;
Natasha Stanglmayr 034 (bottom)

The Publisher would like to thank Theresa Bebbington, Vanessa Bird, Laura Nickoll and Cynthia Kruth for their contributions to the book.